MADELYN I. SAWYER

ADVENTURES OF A FEDERAL AIR MARSHAL

HIRED TO PROTECT

outskirtspress

DENVER, COLORADO

Hired to Protect
Adventures of a Federal Air Marshal
All Rights Reserved.
Copyright © 2012 Madelyn I. Sawyer
v2.0 r1.0

Outskirts Press, Inc.
http://www.outskirtspress.com

ISBN: 978-1-4327-9390-6

Library of Congress Control Number: 2012911210

Outskirts Press and the "OP" logo are trademarks belonging to Outskirts Press, Inc.

PRINTED IN THE UNITED STATES OF AMERICA

For my family, especially my children.

Author's Note

I ENROLLED IN a writing class in January 2012, curious about writing My Life's Story so my children and grandchildren would have a snapshot of what an interesting and intriguing career I've had. *Hired to Protect* took on a life of its own after that first class. The words began tumbling out of me and onto paper as easily as a tumble weed crosses the desert floor on a windy, dry afternoon.

Ruth Herbert, our incredible teacher, and every writer in our class of 2012, were the motivators behind me. I cannot thank them enough.

My family; my Mom, brother, sister, my daughter Monica, son Michael, and their families cheered me on with each chapter's completion. Their excitement kept me on track.

Each chapter's story was re-created as I remembered them best from memory. Throughout this book I intentionally did not use the full names, and in some cases, the actual names of individuals that I have worked with to preserve their anonymity. Special thanks go out to all of my fellow air marshals, thank you for your dedication; especially Ron P. and Earl A., who I flew thousands and thousands of miles with.

My deep felt gratitude goes to Steve Wozenski, a dear friend, who edited and critiqued my drafts from their first pages. Finally, thank you Joan Rogers, editor with Outskirts Press who put the finishing touches on my story. I am so appreciative to everyone for their encouragement and support.

Contents

CHAPTER ONE

Qualification Day

Today was the day my fate would be cast.

AT 3:00 A.M. as I left my room, looking for some solace in the quiet night, the cold, blustery winter wind of Arizona greeted me as a welcome friend. This dry cold wind knew me, knew my gait, and my direction, since I'd made this walk many times before these past four months under cover of darkness.

But this morning I didn't run. I only sauntered along the dirt path, with my wool cap pulled down firmly around my ears, and my thick gloves making sure that my hands stayed warm and flexible for what was to happen in the coming hours. A tear from the cold air rolled quickly down my skin as I made the sign of the cross for protection, along with wishing that the tear was holy water to further give me strength, knowing that I had a critical day before me.

Would I become an elite federal air marshal for the United States government, or would I be returning home unemployed and in despair? My hiring had been swift, as I left my airline employer in St. Croix, United States Virgin Islands with just two weeks' notice to accept the challenge of protecting passengers: those business travelers, tourists, and the airline crews who flew on wings of metal — some for need, some for pleasure, but all in need of protection now.

On December 7th, 1987, PSA 1771 crashed near Cayucos,

California after taking off from the Los Angeles International Airport. This intentional crash had created a void in the aviation security arena that needed to be filled quickly.

Aviation experts on TV said the impacts, looking like large wounds in the earth, possibly made by the landing gear, were in stark contrast to the hilly green countryside of San Luis Obispo County on the Central Coast of California. Eyewitnesses later said the plane was completely intact until it crashed; un-burnt paper was flying everywhere as small aircraft fuel fires began burning on the ground. You could see by the pictures on the television screen that no one had survived this crash.

Several days later, I read that a recently terminated airline employee using his airline credentials had bypassed the security screening checkpoint at LAX and boarded a Pacific Southwest Airlines flight (PSA 1771) that flew daily from Los Angeles to San Francisco. He boarded this specific flight because his manager, who had recently terminated him for petty theft for taking $69 from in-flight cocktail receipts, always flew on this flight, catching a ride every day for his commute to and from home. Sadly, yesterday their souls, along with twenty-six others on board, sailed to heaven, where from 22,000 feet they were doomed to die as their aircraft plummeted to the ground and crashed at airspeed of almost 700 mph.

The terminated airline employee, whose airline badge wasn't surrendered when he was fired, had concealed in his carry-on bag a loaded .44 Magnum that he had recently borrowed from a friend. An airline employee out for revenge was something most of us who had been around aviation for a while could not comprehend, for we were family, and we all looked out for one another as we flew amid the skies of our chosen careers. I read the article with rapt attention, stunned, saddened, and knowing somehow that I wanted to get involved.

Now today, several months after that tragic news, I had hopes of joining that elite cadre who could protect innocent lives.

As a former Navy Air Traffic Controller, and airline employee for many years, I was the perfect candidate. Blonde, blue-eyed, standing five foot eight inches tall, one hundred and twenty-eight pounds, I was fit, intelligent, and savvy. I was ready to serve. "Okay, Maggie Stewart," I said to myself as I walked back toward the dorms, "You've got this. They don't call you 'Mad Dog Stewart' for nothing. Just relax — you know who you are, and know you are damn good at what you do." So much for the pep talk; now I had to perform.

Everyone in FAM school gets a nickname — that is, if you're liked. I earned mine one day during a training run with my team early on in basic training. We had to run a mile and a half in under twelve minutes. I've been a distance runner since high school, but I was never fast. I always trailed the pack with a smile on my face as I felt the wind and sun warming up my skin, with a light sweat forming underneath my tee shirt. I was the dreamer in the group, never imagining that running speed might someday be vital to my career.

So running fast was not in my vocabulary — until now. Now my career depended on it! So during basic training, I ran with total determination. Every single day I ran, trying to imagine that I was pursuing bad guys, chasing evil before it could chase me down. I managed to outrun everyone in my fourth week of training, shouting along the way like a madwoman on steroids. I gave it my all – and "Mad Dog" emerged that day like a hungry coyote howling for food, and knowing she might have to fight to keep it.

Now, today at 0800 hours, when the Arizona sunrise had just peaked, I needed to conjure up that determination once again. I needed to find that coyote hunger. It was qualification day: a day filled with running, shooting, climbing, and outwitting the decoys in the airplane mock-up. This day was mine!

Our dorms were spacious and lavish, decadent actually, in comparison to the open, loud, and cramped barracks that I lived in for seven weeks immediately after I joined the Navy some five-plus years ago now. So having a private room to sleep and work in with a two-person bathroom was like the Ritz Carlton to me. My roommate — or bath mate, in this case — didn't completely share my enthusiasm, but our differing opinions went pretty much unnoticed.

Colleen was brushing her long wiry brown hair, still tangled from the night's sleep she had just woken up from, when I walked in the door. She greeted me by way of a grunt — no coffee yet — and a rolling of her big brown eyes to indicate that yes, she was awake and would be out of the bathroom soon. I laughed and said good morning while taking off my cap and warm gloves, and added, "Take your time." I had already stopped at the mess hall, gotten a cup of coffee for both of us, and used the ladies' room there. Her eyes lit up with glee when she saw the second cup of steaming French Roast, which she immediately knew was for her.

Colleen was from the New York office; I was going to be from the Los Angeles office. I was fortunate enough when I got hired out of Puerto Rico to be able to return to my home state of California. I had been away from my twin sister, my older brother, and parents for almost four years now, so I was elated to be able to finally get back to my family, friends, and the beaches that I loved so much when I was growing up in Southern California.

Colleen's tough voice, with her deep New York accent, could overwhelm a room when she made up her mind to be heard. And she was the best shot of anyone in our class. She was an FBI agent, working at a desk job when the Pan Am tragedy struck and, like me, wanted to be part of the team. So she left the FBI and joined the Federal Aviation Administration (FAA) where the air marshal program was managed. She was perfect. She sailed through her background and psychological testing back in New York, as I did in Los Angeles, and was well on her way to being top of the class in firearms proficiency. Today would be her proving ground as well. She too was ready.

We gave each other a hug, and a high five, and then we bounded for the door, coffees in hand, walking side-by-side to the outdoor track, which was a paved road, where we were scheduled to check in at 0800 hours with the rest of the team.

As we walked up, several of the team members were already

there. You could see the tension in everyone's posture and attitude – we were ready to be called "federal air marshals." As everyone arrived in dribs and drabs we could feel the excitement, like static electricity in the dry desert air; it crackled and sparked as all twenty-four of us gathered for our first qualification of the day, which was the one-and-a-half-mile run.

Our trainer, Mack, was there waiting and watching all of us from the sidelines. He always did his stealth-like observation of us as we interacted in groups while preparing for one of our training runs, swimming endurance tests, or seeing who could levitate or climb over twelve-foot wooden walls in a torrential rainstorm.

Mack walked up to our group once he was sure everyone had gathered and everyone was sufficiently nervous. He was a twisted soul in that sense. He was tall, thin, and looked older than his fifty-five years on this planet. He had an incredibly pock-marked face, burnt skin, and dry thin lips. He was constantly applying Chap Stick to his lips, as if they would never be moist again on their own.

He began hollering out roll call and we individually hollered back our names in response, followed by the word "present." Mack told us — well, ordered us — from day one, to "Shout out your last name ONLY and follow it with the word 'present,' or I'll count you absent!" His former US Marine Corps training had embedded that sergeant's approach to discipline and he was going to be absolutely sure that it was carried forward to his cadre. And Mack was very suc-cessful at everything he did.

"Okay, here's the drill," said Mack. "It's the same course you've been running since you got here four months ago. It's the same flat out-and-back course you've become so familiar with. The only dif-ference now is that IT COUNTS! It's all asphalt, marked only by the outer yellow lines on each side of the road. Fred, here, my assistant coach, will be at the turnaround point to make sure nobody turns around short of the mileage marker."

He took a deep breath and continued. "Run like hell toward Fred, turn around, and run like hell back to me – simple, yes? Is everyone ready to run?" It was not a question.

Mack turned around and glared at "Red Dave" and growled, "So are you planning to run this morning with that cigarette hanging out of your mouth?" Red Dave nodded.

"Okay," said Mack as he turned around, "let's get this race over with. Line up, everyone, and get ready to charge." I lined up beside Colleen, made the sign of the cross, smiled, and shook my hands out to relax. As Mack blew his whistle loud and long, and clicked his stop watch, it became very clear that our quest to become federal air marshals had begun.

The whistle blast faded as pounding feet slapped the pavement with a force creating loud noises like a thundering pack of people running for their lives. I knew my pace was too fast going out, but I'd be damned if I slowed down. I could feel my lungs pulling in the cold, crisp morning air both through my mouth and my nostrils. But I just kept running blindly down the paved road toward Fred. Fred was at the halfway mark, my first goal of the morning. "Just get to Fred, Maggie."

I didn't look left or right. I just pounded the ground and moved forward as fast as I could. I almost felt out of control, but I knew my size-nine shoes would carry me to the end, since they'd been my aides on every training run since day one. I would retire them soon, but not today.

I found Fred, high-fived him as I turned around, and headed back toward Mack, and the finish line. Fred shouted out my split time of 5:35. Five minutes and thirty-five seconds! Yes! I was ahead of my goal by sixty-five seconds. I needed an overall time of twelve minutes to ace this portion of the qualification. And if I kept up this pace, I'd make it.

No bands, no fans, no big banner at the finish line, but it was one of the most exhilarating races of my life. I was exhausted, but I pushed on and ran faster. I could see Fred now. I could hear him shouting at me. I could see the finish line. I raced past Bob and Marc. I could see the sweat pouring off their faces, their hair dripping as they raced for their lives as well. I crossed the finish line a split second ahead of them.

I stumbled forward, knowing I had beaten the twelve-minute demon. My legs wobbled as I walked and tried to catch my breath. My heart was screaming inside my chest, not really believing that the race was complete and it was okay to relax now.

For a few precious moments I basked in my own glory, catching my breath, and then I forced my rebellious legs to start running back toward Fred so I could catch up with some of my teammates and help bring them home.

Big Earl was one of the nicest guys in the world. He must have weighed 250 pounds, with a balding head, big bright blue eyes, and a laugh like Santa Claus'. Big Earl was tough as nails, but would give you the shirt off his back if you asked for it. We were both from the Los Angeles office, so I knew I would be seeing a lot of him in the years to come. I went back to find him. What Big Earl didn't like to do was run; he had way too much body mass to find any pleasure in running, whether recreational or career-related.

Big Earl had about half a mile to go when I got to him. He was lumbering down the road, creating mini earthquakes as his feet pounded the pavement, and you could tell he was tired, but not even close to giving up. He too knew the stakes were high, and he wanted to be an air marshal more than anything in his life. So I ran up beside him and started my banter. "Come on, Big Earl; come on, buddy — we're going to pick up the pace just a little bit." He nodded, that short, curt head nod that runners do to communicate that they've heard you, or seen you, but they don't move away from their running form in any manner. So a head nod is all you get.

We moved along, falling into a swift rhythm, Big Earl following my lead as I slowly increased the pace. We both saw the finish line, and both saw Fred waving his hands wildly in the air, as if that would magically get us there quicker. I shouted out that it was time to "hit it," and we blasted off like bats out of hell. Fred clicked the stop watch and shouted out "11:58" as we crossed the finish line. Big Earl had finished the race with two seconds to spare. He was in!

Everyone had finished in less than twelve minutes, and our class of twenty-four was still intact. Fred told us all to head to the mess hall and get something to drink, and be sure stretch along the way. Our next instructor would come give us our next task in about fifteen minutes. As we slowly sauntered away, Mack hollered out to no one in particular, "Good job."

Heading toward the mess hall, Colleen and I compared notes. We still felt pumped up from the adrenaline rush created by running the race of our lives. We instinctively knew that the next phase of our qualification would be at the pistol range. This was without a doubt Colleen's best event. She was quick on her feet, steady, and could aim at just about anything from any distance and hit it. I was as much in awe and jealous of her shooting abilities as she was of my running.

I was a proficient shooter as well, but I didn't possess the speed that Colleen had. And speed coupled with accuracy was of utmost importance when you were inside an aircraft, flying at cruising altitudes between thirty-one and forty-one thousand feet and suddenly having to defend the flight crew from hijackers.

Fortunately for me, over the past few months, several nights a week after dinner, Colleen had helped me increase my firing speed by overseeing "dry firing" drills, which recreated firing a weapon from the standing and kneeling positions. In return, I would work out with Colleen, doing various fitness routines to build strength and stamina for the physical fitness portion of our training program.

She looked over at me, put her hand on my shoulder and said, "I know you are ready for this, Maggie. Just keep scanning your target area at all times, maintain even trigger control, trust in your abilities, and don't let the flying brass distract you!"

That was easier said than done. Flying brass! I'm a lefty, so I shoot left-handed. When everyone is lined up on the firing line ready to commence firing, the right-handed shooter would be inches away from my extended left firing arm. This scenario always allowed me to have the pleasure of being a little closer to the recoil noise of the shooter on my left, and to the flying brass that sometimes smacked into my protective glasses or flew down the front of my shirt. Either place it landed, hot flying brass was not what you wanted on qualification day.

Upon our arrival at the mess hall our team was greeted by Kevin, our range master. He was ahead of schedule and waiting for most of us. He informed us that we would be spending the rest of the day with him at the range and then in the aircraft mock-up. He told us, as Mack did, to get something to eat and drink, and be at the range at 1100 hours. "Go get into your range gear, too, while you're taking a break."

"It's time for Phase Two," Colleen said as we stood impatiently in line at the mess hall to get something to eat. I opted for a roast beef sandwich with mustard, onions, and lettuce on wheat bread and an orange soda soft drink. I grabbed an enormous calorie-riddled chocolate chip cookie, too.

Everyone gulped their food down in silence, half-chewing their food before swallowing, in an attempt to get out of the mess hall as quickly as they arrived. I was no exception. I was nervous, but confident because just like running, I'd practiced a lot. I'd been to the range every day for the past four months and had shot thousands of 9mm rounds. "Mad Dog would emerge once again." Another pep talk, and another time to perform.

Kevin, our range master, was short, stocky, with thin blond hair, and green eyes that you could hardly see because he squinted so deeply that his eyes were barely visible. He was a man who enjoyed silence, which I always thought was odd since he lived and breathed firearms which, all things considered, were pretty darn noisy. But he was silent most of the time, except to holler out instructions, warnings, or curses when someone screwed up. And it was Kevin's way or the highway. We'd hear that daily, his mantra, his way or the highway, and it was our greatest fear when we were on Kevin's range. "Follow my orders, or I'll send your sorry asses home!" Kevin would holler almost every time we were at the range.

There were twenty-four in our class and room for only twelve shooters at a time at the range. So we drew straws for who would qualify first and who would get to clean up loose brass while waiting to shoot. I was fortunate enough to shoot first.

Our qualifications consisted of shooting paper silhouette targets from close range, double taps to the head, single tap to the main body, then moving back further and further away from the targets as instructed by the range master. All positions of firing were timed, and accuracy was not only critical, but expected. It was pretty much demanded that all of your ammo find the "bull's-eye" each and every time. No pattern targets allowed, just one neat little hole that grew larger and larger as the bullets hit the bull's-eyes with precision and deadly force.

The pace was rapid fire and move, rapid fire and move, farther and farther away from the target, rapid fire and move. Precision was critical because we were training to defend the lives of passengers and crew members onboard aircraft that were in essence flying tin cans that didn't like projectiles moving at one thousand feet per second punching through them. Making a mistake inside a tin can, fondly referred to as an aircraft, was not highly recommended.

Our range master screamed out our names and told us which lane and line to stand behind. I was ordered to go and stand at lane number seven at the three-yard line. I was nestled between Big Earl on my left and Colleen to my right. Our weapons were holstered, our now-sweaty hands at our sides, eye and ear protection in place, and additional clips of ammunition easily accessible. As we lined up, you couldn't hear a pin drop with the ear protection on, but you sure could hear your heartbeat pounding away as if you'd just run a marathon in record-breaking time. "So this is it," I said. "Maggie Stewart, just stay calm, move faster than your normal turtle's pace and forget about everything else. It's all going to be just fine."

The range master shouted "Fire in the hole," and the starting gun went off. Within split seconds, shots fired with a thundering roar as twelve semi-automatic Glocks went off simultaneously. Hot casings went flying everywhere, hitting the ground in front, behind, and beside us like hot raindrops racing to the earth. You could hear them sizzling as they flew through the air before they hit the pavement.

"Cease fire and holster your weapons," commanded the range master. We were directed to the next firing position, and again shots rang out as bullets made their way down to their intended targets. I didn't dare look at my target. I kept my eyes to the ground, ensuring that my firearm was in a safe position before we were directed to holster them and move to our next position. We all moved quietly and with precision. This process was repeated five times in rapid succession, which unfortunately gave us barely enough time to breathe in the warm sage-scented desert air.

Almost before it began it was over. Everyone was again commanded to holster their firearms, and when the range master called the line safe we were to walk down to the three-foot firing line and stand with our hands at our sides and wait for Kevin to score our targets. The wait was grueling, but in reality we could tell quickly by the target positioning if we were going to qualify or not. The closer the bullet holes to the bull's-eye, the higher your score.

I was in lane seven, so I had to wait about fifteen agonizing minutes before Kevin got to my target. One by one he counted the bullet holes in my silhouette and silently recorded his findings at a snail's pace on his clipboard. He certainly was not in a hurry to release us from the range or tell us our fate. When he was finished, he turned and nodded, and said that I had qualified to go onto the next phase of the firearms testing. Not only did I qualify, I qualified as an "expert shooter." Even the ammunition casings saw that "Mad Dog Stewart" was ready, and left me the hell alone as they tumbled past me during my qualification test.

The pistol range qualifications were complete. Again, our team remained fully intact and ready for one more challenge. The team of twenty-four walked immediately over to the B-737 mock-up for the final phase of firearms and tactical training qualifications.

The B-737 that we were about to board came from the boneyard near Tucson, AZ that holds hundreds of aircraft no longer airworthy, but which have plenty of parts that can be resold for other aircraft, or the aircraft can eventually be sold and torn into pieces for scrap metal. This battered shell of a once-graceful flying machine was set aside intact to be raised from the dead like a phoenix to keep a watchful eye over every air marshal trainee that passed through the forward port door seeking his destiny.

Our team gathered outside on the tarmac waiting for further instructions. I stood in place rocking back and forth from my left to my right foot, wearing a black baseball cap, wrap-around sunglasses, training-issued blue short-sleeved cotton button-up shirt, black cotton slacks, and black Nike running shoes. I looked just like everyone else in our issued gear, except my firearm holster was sitting next to my left hip; I was the only left-handed shooter in the group.

The stairs leading to the aircraft were empty. There was no movement inside the aircraft that I could see. The air had warmed to a comfortable eighty degrees and the sky was deep blue, clear, and fresh. I looked across the ramp area and saw the chain link fence with three strands of barbed wire on top, keeping us inside the training facility, along with the saguaro cactus, their massive arms and bodies providing a second level of deterrent, causing anyone thinking of crossing into this restricted area to have a change of mind. These plants of the Sonora Desert can live up to 200 years and grow to 60 feet in height with a hefty weight of up to 4800 pounds. Their bodies are covered with protective spines, as our firearms were, our protective spines against our enemies. I felt at home among these great giants; I was honored to walk on the ground in which they grew. I personally wanted to protect people as well as they protected themselves and thrived.

Soon a black bus raced up the tarmac, stopping just a few feet from the aircraft stairs. The bus doors opened and dozens of people quickly climbed the portable stairs and disappeared into the aircraft without a word being spoken. The last person off the bus was our range master, Kevin. He was dressed completely in black and carried a clipboard in his right hand, letting it swing back and forth as he walked toward us. "Time for Phase Three," Colleen said. She had stepped up beside me, as I was pondering the beauty of the mighty saguaro, reminding me that a final challenge lay ahead.

Kevin appeared as if from nowhere and began flipping through his clipboard and calling our names one by one, telling us to stand easy, and not to go anywhere until he told us to.

This part of the firearms qualifications was the tactical training and would be critical to our abilities to remain in the federal air marshal program from this point forward. This training was given only once, was fast-paced, and had to be executed with extreme precision, or you would be immediately taken off the aircraft and washed out of the program.

We, the team, would be working in groups, amid an airplane full of passengers, crew members, and the ever-watchful eyes of Kevin and his assistant. Today they would not carry firearms, but something more lethal: a clipboard that would record our shots and tactical precision and eliminate us quickly if we didn't execute our teamwork, shoot at the enemies who were aboard the aircraft, and protect the cockpit and its crew at any cost.

Kevin called out to all of us to begin the boarding process. He explained that the ammunition we were receiving as we left the range was rubber bullets with tiny amounts of paint located in tips of the 9mm bullets. When they hit their intended targets the rubber bullets would explode, leaving tiny blobs of paint where they struck. And Kevin warned that it would sting slightly and probably leave a welt if the bullet struck bare skin, so everyone on the aircraft would be wearing protective goggles and light vests. We were to aim only to the body mass of our intended targets for this training exercise. No head shots were allowed. This made the scenario a little more difficult for us, and we had to demonstrate more discipline, since our practices at the firing range were different. But this was tactical training, and the instructions needed to be followed to the letter or we would face disqualification. As we passed Kevin, he gave each of us a slip of paper that told us who our team members would be and what our seat assignments were. He also advised us that the exercise would commence in five minutes with the blowing of his whistle and shouting of "Commence exercise." When the exercise was over the cabin lights would be flicked on and off and he would blow his whistle and shout the command "Cease fire."

I took my seat assignment, first class, closest to the cockpit, and noted who my team members would be. We all had been trained in tactical procedures, so we knew what we were responsible for by our seating location. So once again I said to myself, "Okay, Maggie; pep talk number three, girl. You got this."

The mock-up B-737 was a shell of its former self. The paint on the outside of the aircraft had long lost its luster, for the aluminum was dull, baked, and sad- looking from sitting for years in the hot desert sun. Once you climbed the stairs on the aircraft, you immediately noticed that the forward galley no longer had the capability or equipment to feed anyone, since the serving carts were nonexistent, the coffee pots missing, and not a single serving tray was stacked neatly on the countertops. The framework was the only remaining evidence that a galley ever existed here. The cabin was lit, but mainly by light that leaked in from the dust- crusted portals known as windows. The seats were covered in red and blue upholstery that looked older than my ninety-year-old grandmother's sofa that she refused to part with. But for what we needed, this airplane was fully functional and ready for protection.

I immediately sat down on the dirty, worn seat, placing my federal air marshal (FAM) bag, which was an inconspicuous-looking fanny pack, where I was trained to place it. I looked to the right and left at the passengers beside me and the crew member standing in front of me, who was giving a safety briefing on exit procedures in case we needed to evacuate the aircraft even though we were safely parked in the Sonora Desert, tires flat on the airport tarmac, no operating engines to get us airborne even if we wanted to. But safety was of utmost concern and we listened as the evacuation instructions were recited to us by the crew member.

Once she was seated, the cabin got very quiet. There wasn't any air conditioning working, so the cabin warmed up quickly. I could feel a trickle of sweat begin to form on my forehead as I waited for the exercise to begin. And it didn't take long before I heard loud noises and screaming voices coming from the back of the aircraft.

The shouting grew louder and more pronounced as I heard people screaming above the chant of the would-be hijacker telling everyone to put their heads down and their hands on top of the seats. I heard the stomping of feet running up the narrow aisle of the B-737 toward the cockpit that I knew my team and I were entrusted to protect. My partner behind me said, "Go, I've got your back," and I immediately knew I had to get into the empty galley directly in front of me. I was seated in the first aisle seat, just aft of the galley. I needed to move quickly, low and fast, with my firearm in front of me, my arms slightly down so I could clear my seat and not be immediately seen. I reached into my bag, grabbed my Glock, undid my seatbelt, slid off the seat, and moved around the corner to the galley with lightning speed. I looked left and right to make sure none of the hijackers had reached my position, or worse yet, that there was a sleeper watching and waiting to see if there were any law enforcement personnel onboard. My movement into the galley went unnoticed, except by my partner, who was seated one row behind me and was now pretending to be a passenger complying with the shouting commands of the hijacker.

I dared to peek out from the galley to see two menacing-looking men rapidly moving up the aisle, shouting commands and slapping passengers on the backs of their heads as they passed each row. The passengers were yelling, the hijackers were yelling, and the flight attendants stranded at the back of the aircraft had horrified expressions etched into their faces as they watched the attack unfold.

When the hijackers reached row eleven and came closer to the front of the aircraft, one of our team members stood up and shot the hijacker with a rubber bullet in the middle of his back. One down, one to go — or were there more than two hijackers? The second hijacker ran faster toward the cockpit, and my partner stood and shot him in the chest with a rubber bullet that oozed green paint. I was still hidden in the galley. I steadied my firearm on the wall, waiting for additional hijackers to appear. By now everyone was screaming and shouting.

Then a woman who was sitting right next to my partner jumped up and shot my partner with a rubber bullet that oozed yellow paint, and began climbing over him in her attempt to move toward the cockpit. Without having any time to react, I repositioned slightly, aimed, and shot this hijacker center mass in her chest. The rubber bullet hit the intended target, and green paint oozed once again to show that the target was down. I scanned from side to side to see if anyone else was trying to take over the flight. That's when the lights began to flicker and Kevin's whistle blasted its loud and long shrill, music to my ears, and the passengers began clapping in both relief and elation that this exercise had come to a close.

Kevin announced over the PA system that the exercise was complete and asked for a show of hands if anyone was injured. No hands went up. Thankfully, everyone was safe. The role-playing passengers and crew members were thanked and excused to exit the hot, stench-filled aircraft. Kevin shook each and every volunteer's hands as they departed the aircraft. If it were not for their participation, this exercise would have been useless.

The remaining twenty-four trainees moved forward toward the front of the aircraft to begin their debriefing with Kevin and the coaches that were stationed throughout the aircraft during the exercise. Three trainees, Lynn, Ross, and Carl, had paint on their shirts; two had yellow paint and one had green paint. The green paint meant someone had shot the wrong target, and two trainees had been shot by a hijacker, as indicated by the yellow paint stains. This was where the coaches came into critical play since they were stationed throughout the aircraft and were the official eyes and recorders of the scenario. What they recorded was the "official record" for the exercise and could not be changed or modified once committed to paper. No "under the black hood" review, just what the coaches saw and recorded. The other coaches, like Kevin, had clipboards and they recorded the tactical scenario as it played out inside the aircraft from the minute Kevin's whistle sounded to when the cabin lights flickered at the end.

Lynn and Ross were seated near one another at the rear of the aircraft and they were both shot by hijackers before they rose from their seats. Lynn had been glancing down at a magazine and Ross had just rushed from using the lavatory and was just barely seated when the hijacking exercise began. They were immediately advised that they had failed this exercise because they were not in their tactical positions of readiness when the scenario began. Both of them were being released from the program then and there. Carl's shirt had green ink on it, indicating that he had been shot by a fellow team member. The coach monitoring this section of the aircraft cabin advised the group that Willis had shot Carl before he could get a clear shot at the hijackers; the coach leading this discussion felt that Willis had been nervous, therefore taking a shot prematurely. Willis too was immediately advised that he had failed the exercise and was being released from the program.

The three stunned and mortified trainees forfeited their firearms, protective gear, and magazines, and were escorted quickly off the aircraft by one of the coaches along with two security agents from the training facility. It was a brutal departure, a harsh reality that this was serious business.

As the remaining twenty-one of us deplaned, I looked up into the Arizona sky and saw the broad wings of a soaring vulture circling overhead searching for dinner next to the now lifeless and empty aircraft. I vowed never to allow any human vulture to prey or attempt to bring harm to anyone that I was hired to protect, for I knew now that I was to become a federal air marshal.

CHAPTER **TWO**

Graduation Day Surprise

AFTER A LONG, tense, and stressful qualification day I caught up with Colleen and rest of the team at the base watering hole. This bar was usually hopping since it was the only bar around, and this Friday night was no exception. I wished I had part ownership in the place, because I was positive that this place was going to be making a ton of money tonight. The drinks were going to flow on this Friday night, along with the stories flowing rapidly between lips as they were repeated over and over again. And by the time the weekend was over their tales would soar as high as the tail of the aircraft we soon would be flying aboard.

I was exhausted, exhilarated, and wired beyond words. The adrenaline was flowing. From everything I'd experienced so far and have been taught in some of our training classes that flying high, then crashing after a high threat incident was very much the norm. I sat down, as a glass of red wine magically appeared before my eyes. I smiled in delight, and looked around the bar to see who bought me a drink. Big Earl looked at me from the other end of the bar, tipped his whisky glass toward me, and shouted out his thanks for me saving his butt today during the run. I tipped my glass back in return and shouted back, "Any time, buddy; any time." I swirled the wine in its glass and smelled it before I took my first sip. Why on God's earth I did that, I will never know because the house wine served there was swill, but at least it had the price tag of swill too. So you really couldn't complain much...besides, this was a celebration, not a day to gripe!

The country music of Reba McEntire, Kenney Rogers, and other popular country singers grew louder and louder, dimming out the general conversation. No one was dancing; mostly everyone was standing swaying slightly while the music played, but more absorbed in the conversations taking place. For today was an epic day. At the training facility and in the bar tonight the men outnumbered the ladies. The three remaining women had rebuffed the advances of these guys so many times that everyone finally figured out we're all the same; just some of us were gals and some guys. For the past couple of years I'd been in a monogamous relationship with a hunk of a guy whom I adored. It had been six months since I'd seen Jerry, so I was looking forward to seeing him in Los Angeles in a few weeks.

After a couple of glasses of wine, I could finally feel myself beginning to unwind, so I let my colleagues know that I was calling it a night and heading for my room. Classes began again Monday morning at 0730 hours for one more week of training. However, this training was different — intriguing, really; for all of the classroom briefings were either from Federal Aviation Administration (FAA) Security Intelligence Specialists from Washington, DC; or the Federal Bureau of Intelligence (FBI) from Virginia. And we heard rumors that a "think tank group" contracted by the FAA might be here, as well. Everything this week would be classified and could not be discussed except within the air marshal cadre we would be flying with in the months ahead. I was in dire need of a couple of good nights' sleep before Monday morning. I walked out of the bar into the cool night air with a sense of accomplishment, determination, and relief. I had passed my training and would soon be heading west to California.

Monday morning came with lightning speed. After Friday night's partying, doing laundry and cleaning my room on Saturday was dull in comparison, but necessary. Sunday started with early-morning Mass, followed by a long, glorious hike in the mountains near Bisbee,

AZ. Without a doubt, I was unprepared for the alarm blast that awakened me at 0445 with a jolt. I hit the snooze button once and fell immediately back to sleep, only to be reminded nine minutes later that it was still Monday morning and time to get my butt out of bed or forfeit my morning run. Reluctantly, I rose early and went for my pre-dawn run. A chill was still looming in the air, yet it was beginning to warm up since our arrival on Groundhog Day, February 2nd, 1989. February and March had passed as quickly as a sandstorm does that charges across the desert floor in the Southwest. April was showing the first signs of warming — warming that meant it was time to say farewell, like so many of the snow birds that travel back and forth to escape either the cold or the heat. Now our season here was almost complete, and it was time for us to migrate our separate ways. But like all flocks of birds, we'd all meet again to fly as one.

With my three-mile run complete, I showered, got dressed, and headed to the mess hall to find a hot cup of coffee, boring bowl of oatmeal, and a delicious banana. I didn't particularly care for oatmeal. "But it's really good for you," I kept telling myself. Plus I found it kept me full most of the morning. I'm not much of a morning person to begin with, and eating doesn't appeal to me at all much before 10:00 in the morning. But here by 10:00 a.m. we'd done pool evacuation exercises, firing range time, a two- to three-mile run, coupled with book work, so it was imperative that something be placed in your stomach if you wanted to maintain any level of energy. So I began eating hot oatmeal with brown sugar and a tad bit of half and half in it every morning, with a banana and two cups of coffee.

I grabbed my serving tray and empty coffee cup, and progressed forward with subdued greetings along the way to the kitchen staff. I placed my oatmeal and banana on my tray, found the first available coffee urn, and poured my first cup of coffee for the day. I turned toward the tables and saw Colleen sitting and quickly demolishing a huge plate of food. As I walked up to the table, I said, "I swear that I've never seen anyone eat as much as you can, this early in the morning." She smiled, and started to say something but changed her mind as some scrambled eggs tumbled out of her mouth, and her manners kicked in and she remained silent until she has swallowed her eggs.

"I know, I know," she said, "but I just get hungry in the morning. My dad always said to me in the morning to eat up because who knows where you're going to find your next meal? I have no idea why he always said that, but after years of eating a lot in the morning it just stuck with me all these years."

Well, maybe that was where I got my lack of eating in the morning from. I was raised by my dad and my grandmother from the time I was eight years old, and Grandma would get us up just in time to eat breakfast, and then rush us out the door to go get on the school bus. Why we had to stand outside to wait for the bus always puzzled me since the bus stop was on the same corner as our three- bedroom, two-bath downstairs apartment was, but that's another story. Anyway, the ride from the bus stop to school was almost an hour and the last thing I wanted to worry about was finding a bathroom. So my grandmother would fuss and fuss at me, pointing her finger at me, trying to convince me that I needed to eat more. But I never did, and I never had to have that school bus stop, either. Eventually Grandma Irene finally stopped pestering me, and began placing only an English muffin with orange marmalade on my plate in those early- morning hours before my long, tedious, and sometimes dreaded bus ride to school. We had met in the middle, my Grandma and I. Not that I understood that then, but I do now, and it was her way of helping me and telling me how much she loved me.

With great anticipation, we all walked back into the classroom, several inches taller than last week, for all of our accomplishments last Friday had made us all very proud. Graduation ceremonies were being held this coming Friday, so the next four days would pass with rapid speed. Our intellectual senses were piqued this week in anticipation of hearing the classified information detailing the reasons for and solidifying the importance of our future missions.

In the classroom this week, we would all come to fully understand the job responsibilities of being special agents when working at airports inspecting the airport, airlines, and cargo facilities to ensure they were in compliance with federal regulations. This ground work demanded of us that we not only have a full understanding of the regulations, but an ability to build and foster cooperation and team-work among aviation professionals that at times did not agree with the regulations that needed to be enforced. So the work could be challenging, confrontational, and difficult at times.

When working at an airport we were special agents and we did not carry a firearm; we enforced regulations with a pen and notepad. And you know the saying that a pen, if used correctly, can be dead-lier than a bullet. From everything that I had heard from the class that graduated before me, being a special agent was as much of a chal-lenge as being an air marshal. You needed to know the regulations, be a team player, and write extremely well.

Along with being challenging, it was really interesting and ex-citing. One aspect of the job of special agent was attempting to penetrate screening security checkpoints, and other restricted areas of an airport. You had to attempt to thwart the system by bypassing into "sterile" and "secure" areas undetected. The purpose was solely to see if the security posture of the airline or airport was in compli-ance with federal regulations and safe. I was excited to learn more about this part of my job when I got to my field office in Los Angeles next week. "Here we go — one more week, girl, and you graduate," I thought as I swaggered over to my chair.

Once in the classroom, I sat at the same table and seat that I had been sitting in for months. I was comfortable, content, and anxiously awaiting the lessons to be taught this week.

Our instructor was already standing up at the front of the class, near the window, with a cup of coffee in his left hand, and a thick document in his right hand with a red and white cover on it. He wasn't reading it; he was looking out the window at the morning sky and seemed to be lost in thought, for he didn't acknowledge anyone when they walked in the room or seated themselves. He just stared out the window, as the steam from his hot coffee rose gently into the air and disappeared before our eyes.

After we were all seated, he silently turned and looked at every one of us, staring for a few seconds directly into each of our eyes as if to communicate directly with each of us individually, as he slowly scanned the room. "Congratulations," he said with his firm, radio-quality voice. "Welcome to your last week here and perhaps one of the most important and secretive. No note-taking; just listen up — eyes and ears only this week. Stay engaged; this is important stuff, and the ladies and gentlemen you will meet this week have a vested interest in your ability to understand and act on the information we are about to discuss here."

The classroom door opened as if on cue, and the first guest, an intelligence analyst from the Federal Aviation Administration, Aviation Security Division, walked into the room.

Day after day the classified briefings continued, solidifying our understanding that the terrorism threat against US targets was real and that it wasn't going away anytime soon. We were afforded the most valuable, sensitive, and classified information briefings imaginable. Keeping this information closely held was our cadre's mandate.

After the last security briefing late Thursday afternoon, it was time to head back to our rooms, pack, relax, and prepare for an early-morning rise and shine. Our last day of training was to end early tomorrow morning, Friday, April 13th with an unpretentious ceremony where each trainee would be presented, by the Aviation Security Office Director, our federal air marshal credentials, badges, authorization to carry, and his solemn blessings.

The blasting squawks of my Sandhill Cranes alarm jolted me awake. I never imagined that I could sleep so soundly when I closed my eyes just a few hours earlier having finally packed and spent the evening chatting with my colleagues and anticipating the future. Finally Friday the 13th was upon us and it was time to graduate.

I raced through my morning routine like a strike of lightning racing toward the earth. It was time to escape this training environment and fly our first mission. We had spent four months training, learning, and anticipating the day we would be become an elite cadre of air marshals. And today was the day!

I was a nervous ball of anticipation by the time I arrived at our classroom where roll call would be taken before we walked our final walk to the auditorium, where it all began, to graduate. My midnight-blue 4-wheel drive Jeep Sport, with off-road tires, was parked nearby, packed, and I was ready to find Interstate 8 and head west. "Farewell cactus and hello Pacific Ocean," I said to myself as I walked into the auditorium. Once I left Arizona I was going to spend the weekend with my twin sister, Sylvia, who lived in San Diego, before heading north to Los Angeles to report for work on Monday morning at the Los Angeles Civil Aviation Security Field Office (LAX CASFO) located on the south side of LAX airport property.

Twenty-one graduates, as lucky as a deck cards at a blackjack table in Vegas, sat in the first and second rows of the auditorium, waiting for the director to arrive and the graduation commencement to begin. We spoke among ourselves while we waited; the low murmur of our voices sounded like the slow beating of a perfectly functioning heart: steady, quiet, and calm. You could see that we had all matured, grown stronger, and were already callused in some ways, watching fellow colleagues drop away without one of us looking back; time to move onward was our only focus now.

The Director of Aviation Security, Ray Sword, for the FAA, walked into the room and everyone, as if on auto-pilot, jumped to their feet and stood at attention. We weren't in the military and we weren't rising at Mass when the Father began his cadence up the aisle, but we definitely knew this man's importance and we were compelled to rise as if we were new recruits. It was an unforgettable moment in our young careers.

Director Sword asked us all to be seated and immediately stated how happy he was to be among us and learn of our incredible accomplishments here. He said, in a firm and confident voice, "I am here not only to present the graduating class with their special agent credentials; I am here to present the three top honors of the class for firearms, physical fitness, and academia."

The ceremony was swift and without any fanfare. The three top honors went to the remaining three women in the class: Colleen for firearms, Georgia for academia, and myself for physical fitness. We three ladies had beaten all of the big burly men in our graduating class and, we proudly accepted this recognition by the director.

As the ceremony wrapped up, Colleen, Georgia, and I were asked to stay in the auditorium and have pictures taken with the director with the American Flag as our backdrop. Everyone else began shaking hands with Director Sword, our instructors, and some of the staff support that came into the auditorium to say so long. Our cadre was gone and we three stood beside the director while cameras snapped away, framing and capturing our smiling faces forever.

Once we said our goodbyes, we too began walking toward the front office to officially sign out from the base, turn in our room keys, and then drift off in our different directions toward new adventures.

At the office, I gave my room key to Gladys, signed off on all the required paperwork, and turned to head out of the office when Gladys picked up the ringing telephone on her desk, listened, and then called my name as my hand touched the door handle. "Maggie, there is call is for you, sweetie."

I turned around with a puzzled look on my face, and walked over to take the phone from Gladys's hand. "Thanks," I said. "Hello, this is Maggie Stewart."

Jerry, my boyfriend of two years, said in a very sad and subdued voice, "I'm so sorry, Maggie."

Then a female voice on the other end of the telephone said, "Hello. My name is Rhonda, and I'm your boyfriend Jerry's wife. So don't plan on seeing him anymore, honey." Then the telephone line was disconnected, along with my life as I knew it.

In a split second my facial expression went from looking puzzled to looking shocked. I could feel my head bobbing up and down, at a loss for words. It didn't matter, and I couldn't move my lips to respond anyway. I saw Gladys looking at me with growing concern as she reached out and touched the bent elbow of my arm that was holding the weapon of such traumatic news. Standing there numb, stung, and speechless, I hung up the phone. I gave Gladys a quick hug, said everyone was okay, just some business that needed to be resolved, and I burst from the room like a rocket heading out of the earth's atmosphere. Fortunately for me, when I got to my Jeep everyone one else had already left, already traveling to their destinations. I placed my hand in my jacket pocket, looking for my car keys. I was on my own again, literally alone, and heading west, tears beginning to stream down my face, without a Kleenex to my name.

I started up my Jeep, and sensing my pain, she rumbled, purred, and let me know by the sounds she made that she wasn't going to give my any trouble. She would be the vessel that would give me safe passage across the Mojave Desert in the heat of the day, carrying me safely while the heat of anger began rising in me. "Shit," I said, "men." I flipped on the air conditioner, rolled up the windows, checked the mirrors, buckled my seatbelt, turned, and looking over my right shoulder, saw that I was clear to back out of my parking space. I backed up, turned back around, looked squarely out the front windshield, and headed out of the Marana Air Base parking lot.

As I turned onto Interstate 10, heading north, leaving Marana in the rear view mirror, I wanted to get away from this place, this base, this mess that was in my head. I drove past Elroy, AZ and turned onto Interstate 8 for the 375-mile ride to my sister's house in San Diego. "Well at least I'm getting back to my twin," I said to myself.

As I drove numbly along through the Sonora Desert I thought back to when I was working for a subsidiary of American Airlines in St. Croix, US Virgin Islands, as the Director of In-flight Services, and how I had met Jerry one bright, gorgeous Caribbean day on the ramp just outside of the terminal. He was a lieutenant in the Air Force Reserve and he flew C-130s around the world, tracking hurricanes for the Air Force and National Weather Service. I was running late for my flight and I nearly knocked him down with my roll-on bag as I raced across the tarmac for the jet stairs to board the 51 passenger CV-440. He was the most incredibly handsome man I had ever seen, and I was smitten from the day he smiled at me and said hello as he righted my bag. He was a charmer, a looker, and intelligent.

I should have added resourceful as a verb to describe Jerry too, for a few weeks later as I was sitting in my second story office, with a window view overlooking the south side of the airport ramp, I heard a slight single rapid tap on the window pane. I wondered if birds were playing with me by trying to get into the office to eat the popcorn I had just popped and was munching on when I heard that dull but distinct tap again. I decided to investigate and take a look outside. I rose from my desk and walked cautiously, but curiously, over to the window and looked out and down to the ramp below. Standing there with a handful of rocks was Jerry, smiling up at me, a twinkle in his eye, his light-brown hair gently ruffled by the afternoon breeze off the Caribbean Sea nearby. Little did I know that I should have continued eating my popcorn, while ignoring the persistent tapping on the window. Right then and there our romance began. We walked over to the airport bar that was directly behind the building where I worked on the non-secure side of the airport, and talked and drank until the wee hours of the morning.

Over the next few months I traveled to New Orleans, and he traveled to St. Croix. I love contemporary art, so when we were in New Orleans, we'd visit art shop after art shop, talking quietly together or in a shared conversation with the shop attendee, owner, or sometimes the artist if we had the opportunity.

When we were in St. Croix we walked the beach day after day hand in hand, laughing or quietly smiling. We'd snorkel in the warm clear water at the Buck Island Reef National Monument just offshore from Christiansted Harbor. The fish were abundant here, for I think they knew they were in a place that was protected, and they were free to become our friends as we fed them fish bait that we bought in town.

I flew with him unofficially as an Air Force crew member to

England, the Azores, and all around the Caribbean Islands; visiting Puerto Rico in the Greater Antilles, as we traveled southward into the Less Antilles of St. Thomas, St. Kitts & Nevis, Barbados, and finally Trinidad & Tobago, while he and his crew tracked and analyzed hurricanes. Those were incredibly bumpy flights and I wasn't sure I had used the best judgment in agreeing to go along for those hurricane-hunting flights, but the adventures were grand, and I saw many new places, experiencing different cultures in the world I never imagined. I was in love through and through.

In my mind, these were glorious times, for a few years before I received that fateful telephone call.

I felt angry, and I felt like a fool. "What didn't I see? Come on Maggie. What did you miss, girl?" I said out loud, hoping my Jeep would bring me the answer.

After six hours of analyzing my life and dealing with some stop-and-go traffic as I headed into California, I arrived at my sister's house close to 10:00 p.m. She lived in Pacific Beach, perched up on a hill, in a small two-bedroom, two-bath home, with a peek-a-boo view of the Pacific Ocean. I could smell the salt air as I opened my car door and stepped onto her driveway. It was refreshing to feel the humidity in the air, as heavy as my heart had been these past miles, but I could also feel relief knowing that my sister's warm greeting and smile would be upon me as soon as she opened her front door. And magically, her front door opened and my sister raced out, down the short walkway, and gave me the hug of a lifetime. She rocked me back with her strong arms and looked me up and down and said, "Well, you look pretty darn good, all things considered!" My sister always had a way with words and I didn't know if I wanted to laugh, cry, or spit, I was so worn out. But I was with my sister and I needed her sanctuary this weekend so I could regroup in preparation for my first day.

My sister and I are fraternal twins, born five minutes apart, first her and then me. My Dad named us Sylvia and Maggie, names that have no family history whatsoever. Our middle names are those of our great-aunt and grandmother, Nell and Irene, so those names made sense to us, but not our given names. Our brother, who is two years older, is named Timothy Ian, names with no family ties either, so I guess our dad just wanted to do things his way. This was pretty much the way Dad was in all facets of his life.

My sister was a mechanical engineer by trade and was the smartest person I knew. She could look at something that was broken and figure out how to repair it in a matter of minutes. She'd build things from scratch, taking measurements, and with hand tools create what she desired. She was fun, tough, smart, fit, and my best friend. I hadn't seen her in about a year, so this weekend we would have a lot of catching up to do.

I, on the other hand, was the goof and the dreamer in the family. I was happy-go-lucky in every aspect of my life. I always believed that people would be honest, real, caring and fair. It was a wonder that I had gotten into the line of work I was about to embark upon, but I too could be tough when I needed to be. It was just a side most people didn't see unless they made me angry. But I was passionate about protecting this country, and that passion would be the catalyst that would keep me strong.

As my sister and I walked side by side up the walkway we began chatting nonstop about the drive, graduation, and my jerk of an ex-boyfriend, Jerry.

Inside her warm and cozy house we settled down on the sofa. The fireplace was crackling with a bright and cheery fire, and the view from her almost-ceiling-to-floor windows showed trees swaying slightly in the evening breeze. She had poured us each a glass of wine, brought out a tray of various cheeses, crackers, and fruits. We began feasting, and catching up on life.

My sister had a job at a private surveying firm and was telling me all about the projects she was working on and the Indian artifacts they had just recently found in the city of Imperial off Interstate 8. She clearly loved her job and was really happy to be a surveyor out in the field versus sitting behind a desk every day. It was a magical job for her.

My sister told me all about Bernie, whom she had been dating for just a few months, but everything was going along really well and she hoped I would meet him this weekend. And yes, after the surprise of Jerry being married she immediately called Bernie to confirm that he was indeed a single man. I laughed, as that was such a twin thing, to call him and ask. That type of phone call was our way of watching out for each other; it's just what twins did.

My sister and I polished off a bottle of wine and decided we probably better get some sleep because we both wanted to get up early tomorrow and go to Coronado Beach for an early-morning walk. My sister wasn't a runner, but she could walk for miles and miles and that was perfectly all right with me. Being with my sister, going to the beach, and walking for miles were exactly the things I needed and had hoped we could do this weekend. So off to sleep we went.

Unlike me, my sister is an early riser, so I didn't need my Sandhill Crane alarm to wake me up at 0530. Sylvia opened my door, tapped gently on the door frame and said, "Good morning, coffee is ready." I slowly opened one eye, then the other, feeling the effects of a few glasses of wine and the hectic schedule I had been following these past four months. I wondered why had I agreed to this early-morning rise and shine as I pushed back my covers, shivering while looking for my robe and flip-flops. Her big fat yellow tabby cat, Miss Daisy, was sleeping on one of the pillows where my head was peacefully at rest, and slowly rolled her big cat eyes as me as if to say, "Ha, ha, better you than me, sister." I knew the meaning of the saying "It's a cat's life," now as I murmured under my breath.

Robe and flip-flops found, I made my way to the kitchen by way of a stop at the bathroom and got a look at myself in the mirror. "Yikes," I said to myself, looking at the red eyes and bags, "you look like hell, girl!" I quickly washed my face in the cold water streaming from the sink tap and patted my skin dry with the hand towel that was sitting on the sink's marble countertop.

We had our first cup of coffee at the house, and the second cup we would carry in a thermos with us in the car. My sister always poured water into the cold coffee cups, and then warmed the cups up in the microwave. She would dump the scalding hot water into the thermos and quickly replace the lid on it and let it warm up while we had our first cup of coffee. Starbucks' French Roast and cream, not milk — nothing artificial, but fattening, wonderful, delicious half and half. Coffee at Sylvia's was a ritual, never to be broken, like Catholic wedding vows. My sister's coffee was a treat that stuck in your memory forever. She was a gem and I loved her and her coffee. It was worth getting up this early.

Arriving at the beach at 0630 was worth the early rise as well. The tide was very low, so there were miles and miles of firm sand to walk along with virtually no one around. The sun was still low in the sky; the early morning layer had not yet begun to burn off, and the slightly westerly wind was cool but comfortable. It was heaven to walk along that flat beach, mingling among shorebirds in various stages of winter migration.

My sister is a "birder," so she pointed out to me the differences in colors, shapes, and body sizes among these shorebirds. The Wimbrel and the Long-Billed Curlews were large birds proudly displaying long and curved bills, while the Marbled Godwit had a long bill, but it was straight. I wondered how these birds could walk, much less fly, since their bills looked so out of proportion compared to their bodies. But fly they did, for these birds migrated up and down the West Coast annually, and this morning we were fortunate enough to see them in the final stages of their winter migration. The Sandpipers ran around in frantic disarray when our footsteps got too close, while the Sanderlings didn't grace us at all with their presence, taking off in compact flocks that twisted and turned erratically as they escaped their perceived threat. Offshore, flying gracefully above the surf line, was a group of the ever-present Brown Pelicans. They don't migrate, so our southern California Beaches are always blessed with their graceful beauty.

My sister and I walked nearly five miles to the Mexican border, past the small funky beach city of Imperial Beach, picking up seashells and sand dollars along the way. When we reached the river that divides Mexico from California, we turned around and headed back toward my sister's car. Our legs were tired, but our spirits were lifted, as we welcomed the greetings of others as the beach shores began to fill with surfers, walkers, runners, and human life. I was always glad we got up early and our walks were almost complete by the time others were sipping their first cup of morning coffee.

We spent the rest of the weekend doing chores in preparation for the week ahead. I was heading north up Interstate 5 tomorrow morning in preparation for reporting to work at 0730 on Monday morning. A new job, new beginnings, old boyfriends left behind — but I was near my family again, and they were already supporting me more than they knew. "I am so lucky to have a twin sister," I said to myself. My sister, always the early bird, wanted one last early-morning walk before we parted ways once again. But at least now I lived in California, a mere hundred miles away.

I wanted to go to Mass the next morning, so we decided to walk around her neighborhood instead of driving to the beach. That way we could walk for a few hours and I'd still have time to make 0830 mass at Holy Trinity Catholic Church, which was just a few blocks from my sister's house. It was, as always, our way of figuring out a plan that we both agreed on and allowed us both to do what we needed to do. It's a twin thing, magical and perfect. I love my sis.

Our early walk was done, and Mass was incredible; after I put my overnight bag back into my Jeep, I turned and hugged my sister tightly and told her I'd call when I got to L.A. I was going to stop at my brother's house, for lunch with Tim and his wife Marilyn, and then head to my hotel, The Beach Hotel in Manhattan Beach, CA. It was a little expensive for my new-hire budget, but I needed to stay close to the office to avoid the Los Angeles area traffic jams and I didn't have anywhere else to live at the moment since I didn't know a soul at the LAX field office except for Big Earl, and he was a new agent too.

"I love you, sis," I said as I got into my Jeep.

"I love you too," my sister said. "Don't forget to call when you get to Tim's. I want to know that you are okay."

"Will do, honey."

As I backed out of her driveway, I knew my official adventure had begun. I was a federal air marshal heading for my first post of duty.

CHAPTER **THREE**

The Los Angeles Field Office

THE DRIVE TO Los Angeles, thankfully, was completely uneventful. I had a full tank of gas when I left my sister's house, so I needed to stop only for a restroom break at the rest stop on Interstate 5 near the Marine Corps Base, north of Oceanside. The traffic was very light for a Sunday morning.

I arrived at my brother Tim's house at noon and was greeted with a great big bear hug and a pat on the back. My brother stood 6'1," with an athletic body gained from many years of surfing and wind surfing. His calves were as big as many men's thighs, after decades of hanging onto a sail and flying across the open ocean, skimming the waves of California and Hawaii, his two favorite places to surf and sail. Tim is two years older than my sister and I, and he is a total computer geek. He works with hardware and software, building and maintaining computers for several large corporations throughout his career, and is a wizard from everything I had heard or read about him. Yet he doesn't act like a computer geek at all. To me he's just my big brother, a surfer dude whom I admire very much. The world is his oyster and he is one of nicest guys I know. His laugh is contagious, his bear hugs warm and welcoming, and his smile is always full of glee. We weren't as close to one another growing up as my sister and I were. But twins had a way of making that happen, and I knew he would do anything in the world for me and was always happy to see me.

Marilyn, his wife, hugged me and showed me where to place my shoes after I had taken them off just outside the front door. Their carpet was a perfect shade of white; it looked creamy and brand-new even after several years, and Marilyn intended it to remain that way for many more years to come.

Tim and I sat outside and chatted while Marilyn brought out a beautiful quiche, fresh fruit salad, and French bread. Everything was served on bright cheerful plates that looked perfect on their outdoor patio glass table. Marilyn took great pride in her kitchen and her ability as a culinary artist. I was envious, for I was a great eater, but a terrible cook, so being around their house near meal times was always like going to a five-star gourmet restaurant. Everything was fresh and delicious, with a stellar presentation. I was getting sufficiently fattened up with the marvelous lunch that Marilyn prepared as the birds chirped merrily in the background and the sun was shining brightly high above us in Huntington Beach. It was another picture-perfect day in southern California.

After lunch, while helping Marilyn with the dishes, I talked a little bit about my abrupt break-up with Jerry and my new job. One part of the conversation was melancholy and full of a sense of loss, and the flip side of the conversation was one of pure excitement and moving forward into the future. Marilyn didn't say much, but her nods, smiles, and caring eyes told me all I needed to know. She had listened in her quiet style, supportive and elated for me; she nodded in agreement with me that she too felt I had found a career that would suit me well. She and I knew it was time for me to find some roots.

The kitchen was finally clean, just as the afternoon golf tournament was beginning on Channel Two. It was time for me continue my drive north, just another twenty-five miles to my destination. Hugs came once again at my Jeep's car door from Tim and Marilyn, and as I got into the driver's seat I said, "See you later," and "I'll let you know how everything is going. Love you, and thanks for lunch."

I decided to drive along Pacific Coast Highway, passing through the small communities of Sunset Beach, Surfside, Seal Beach, and then through the larger city of Long Beach, crossing the beautiful span of the Vincent Thomas Bridge that showcased the Los Angeles Harbor and dropped you into the city of San Pedro from its green span of metal.

When we were kids our family lived in San Pedro for a few years aboard a boat in the San Pedro Harbor. My brother, sister, and I learned how to sail before we learned how to ride bicycles. Living aboard a boat was a great adventure for us; we rowed our dinghy up and down every boat dock channel in the marina, sailed in and out of the harbor, fished off the docks, ran amok (I suspect), and smelled the stench of the kelp factory weekly, its pungent and unique odor filling our nostrils for hours before we finally got used to the smell. Week after week we got up early to be driven to school by our mom while our dad went to work at the nearby marina.

After our parents divorced, we moved into a tract home near Gaffey Street on Stalter Street. I barely remember the house, except that it was two stories, and every house on the street looked the same. The front yards were all flattened piles of dirt, and each new owner had to individually design and create their front yard landscapes, as we had to recreate our life's landscape after our parents divorced. My brother was ten at the time, and my sister and I were eight. I didn't understand what had happened; one day we were living in a house, then a boat, and then back into a house in a new city with only one parent: my dad, who worked most of the time, but always ate dinner with us, retiring soon afterward to his bedroom every evening.

As I grew older I began to understand more about how difficult life could be, but back then I can remember only being moved to a different school, and a new set of rules, both at school and at home when my grandmother came to live with us. I vividly remember becoming very self-sufficient, a characteristic that became an asset to me as I grew older. But when I was young I remember it only as feeling alone. Thank goodness I had a twin sister to be near.

I held onto a few good memories; the Wonder Bread Bakery field trip we went on in grade school, the tiny loaf of warm bread given to each student after the tour, the wonderful aroma of that freshly baked bread. Where-oh-where was that bakery? I wondered as I drove down Gaffey to find my way back to Pacific Coast Highway after getting off the Vincent Thomas Bridge.

I made the left turn back onto Pacific Coast Highway and traveled slower over the next ten miles than anywhere else since I had left San Diego earlier in the day. Daylight was beginning to dwindle; dusk would soon be upon us and people were finishing up their busy days of being out on a beautiful Sunday by driving home all at the same time. "Time for patience," I said to myself as I slowly drifted by fast food after fast food restaurant, grocery stores, gas stations, and small strip malls that all looked the same, separated only by different street names and their barely legible addresses. This part of the Greater Los Angeles Area was no less congested than anywhere else in Los Angeles; the only benefit was the cool breezes from the Pacific Ocean just a few miles away.

I arrived at the Beach Hotel twenty minutes later, missing my first sunset, but finding comfort in knowing there were many more to come now that I was back in California. I parked the Jeep, checked in, dropped my bag in my room, and decided to go for a short walk before it got too late.

The Beach Hotel was right on The Strand in the small city of Hermosa Beach, CA. The Strand's sidewalk went for twenty-five miles along the Santa Monica Bay, stretching from the Redondo and Torrance Beach — or what the locals called RAT Beach — twenty-five miles to the north, ending at the famous Malibu Beach. This portion of the Strand had street lights so you could walk to the local small restaurants nearby or get out for exercise in the evening. Back at the beach, going for a walk just couldn't be any better.

I quickly changed into my running clothes, threw on a light jacket since I wasn't use to the ocean breeze, and headed out the door for a quick three-mile run. I had nervous energy to burn and I could hear the ocean waves crashing on the shore as I made my way along the cement strip, passing million-dollar homes, built side-by-side, divided only by each owner's small sidewalk placed neatly between their gigantic and lavish homes. I loved the beach but I never thought I'd want to live in one of these homes, for it was similar to living in a goldfish bowl. Every runner, walker, or bicycle rider would turn and gawk into the enormous windows to see if anyone was home, and if so, what were they doing. The lack of privacy would not suit me at all.

I finished up my walk, stopped at the front desk and asked for directions to the nearest grocery store, went back to my room, grabbed my wallet, and walked two blocks in the opposite direction of my walk, where I found Ralph's Grocery Store, just as the front desk clerk had said. I quickly picked up some fruit, crackers, cheese, a bottle of red wine, Starbucks ground coffee, half and half, Equal sweetener, and a few frozen dinners. The room had a small kitchenette, so I could save some money while I was staying there and eat in the room rather than going out all of the time. I was hoping too that I would eat a hot lunch out every day, either with people from the office or on my own, so my main meal of the day would be lunch.

Back at my room, I put away the groceries, poured myself a glass of red wine, unpacked my clothes, ironed what I was going to wear to work tomorrow, and sat and caught the 10:00 news.

I turned off the TV at 10:30 p.m., took a shower, got my PJs on, and lay down in the soft old creaky hotel room bed. I was on the second story of the two-story hotel, so at least I didn't have anyone in a room above me. Since I had booked the room for a month, they gave me a room at the end of the hall, overlooking the parking lot, but it was quieter and more private. No view, but I could hear and smell the ocean, and that was heaven. I had to admit the room wasn't heaven or a dream suite, that was for sure, but it was relatively inexpensive, right on the beach, and five miles from the field office and two miles from the regional office. I had been assigned to the field office, but was advised that occasionally I would need to go to the regional office too. So for me, it was the perfect place to be until I got my feet on the ground, learned the area better, and saved a little bit more money. "Night, Lord," I said to myself. "Thanks for getting me here — thanks for everything."

I woke up before my alarm went off, to the sounds of cars outside my window, in the parking lot on the ground floor as it began to fill up with workers parking their cars as they began their busy days working in the nearby hotels or restaurants near the Hermosa Beach Pier. The sky to the east was just beginning to turn marvelous shades of red, pink, gray, and light-blue. I quickly got up and put my robe on in an attempt to warm up. My room was very chilly, since I had left the window open all night to hear the calming motion of the ocean pounding against the sand.

I moved the few feet it took to reach the coffee pot in the kitchenette, and turned it on; after filling the empty coffee cup on the counter with water, I placed it in the microwave for two minutes. I went to the restroom, returning in time to hear the microwave buzz, and the two-cup coffee pot had just about finished percolating my morning nectar. My Equal and half and half were sitting on the counter in anticipation of their being added to my steaming cup of coffee. Early-morning coffee was always a treat — and necessary for survival, in my mind.

At 0700 hours I closed and locked my hotel room, went downstairs to the parking lot, and warmed up my Jeep up for a few minutes before I began the five-mile drive north on the Pacific Coast Highway to the Los Angeles Civil Aviation Security Office (LAX CASFO) located on Imperial Blvd., on the west side of the Los Angeles International Airport.

I discovered that even though the commute was short in miles, it took all of the thirty minutes I had allotted myself, because the traffic on Pacific Coast Highway was bumper to bumper, all three lanes in both directors saturated, exhaust fumes streaming out of every car, spitting out a mixture of wet morning dew and gas as if to clear their lungs. I really didn't want to be late for my first day, but I was beginning to worry that I might be.

The designated parking lot for the field office was just about full when I arrived. I learned later that most of the agents started working at 0600 hours so they could avoid some of the traffic congestion that I'd just had the opportunity to experience. I parked in the very back of the lot, hanging from the rear view mirror my temporary vehicle tag, which the security guard had provided me after I showed him my credentials. He confirmed my authorization by looking on a visitor list; he located my name, confirmed once again that I was Maggie Stewart, and granted me access to the parking lot.

I hurried toward the double glass office doors and waited again to be cleared by another security guard, who gave me a temporary access badge with big letters saying "ESCORT" across the top. I was told to wait in the lobby and someone from the field office would come and escort me to the office. I had signed in at exactly 0700, and quietly sat down and waited. I looked down at my black Navy training hand-polished shoes, black slacks, matching black blazer and my light-yellow blouse and felt confident that I was conservative, comfortable, and practically dressed for my first day. I was not sure what to expect, but I wanted to look professional and exude the confidence I felt — well, sort of felt.

Within a few minutes a young woman dressed in black slacks, with a white blouse, nodded to the security guard and began walking toward me. "Hi, I'm Kelly," she said. "I'm the administrative assistant for the manager here, Cindy Clark." She extended her hand and shook my hand firmly.

"You don't mind taking the stairs, do you?" Kelly asked as we headed toward the stairs.

"Oh, not at all," I said. "The more I can walk, the better."

"Okay," Kelly said. "We're only on the second floor, but there are a lot of stairs because our office is above an aircraft hangar. Come on, let's go meet the bosses."

We climbed the stairs in silence. And she was right about the number of stairs. I have always had the habit of counting stairs when I climb them, and a normal set of stairs between floors is twenty. By the time we arrived at the office we had climbed forty-seven stairs, switching back and forth every ten stairs as we climbed up and up. It was a wide stairwell — dull, as you can imagine, with scuff marks all along the walls; some were low and close to the steps, probably made by shoes, while others were higher up on the walls, perhaps made by boxes or other items being carried between the upstairs offices and the ground floor. There were emergency lights dotted along the way close to the ceiling that would be automatically turned on if the fire alarm system were activated.

When we got to the office, again double glass doors separated us from the inner workings of the office. I could feel my heart pounding from the stairwell climb along with the anticipation of meeting my new boss and beginning my first day on the job. Kelly opened the door for me and I stepped into the office and onto carpet that was old, filthy dirty, worn, and bright mandarin orange! Kelly walked up beside me and I knew she had read my mind when she said with a chuckle and a smile, "Pretty awful, isn't it? At least we don't have to worry when we spill our coffee."

"Yep, it's pretty ugly," I said, nodding my head in agreement as we walked toward the manager's office. Along the way, agents looked up from their desks and nodded as I passed. The office was an open bay with only two private offices: one for the manager, and one for the supervisor. A makeshift kitchen area, massive filing cabinets, and I guessed about twelve desks filled up the open pit area. Fortunately, with all of this furniture only small areas of carpet were exposed to the human eye.

When we got to Cindy's office, Kelly tapped on the door frame, and Cindy, sitting at her desk, with her head bent over paperwork, looked up and silently waved us into her office space.

Kelly motioned me to sit down as she began literally backing up toward the office door. As Kelly turned about-face to leave, Cindy asked her to have Rob come to her office now.

Then Cindy, barely looking at me, said she would be right with me and quickly looked back down to her stack of paperwork, and began scribbling notes and signatures on various pieces of paper and folders.

I quietly waited and began looking around her office, wondering what the various pictures and plaques were about, for her office walls were covered with wall decorations of every size, shape, and color.

Some looked like professional plaques; others looked like personal artwork. Her office was messy, but somehow I think she knew where every piece of paper was. She was well-dressed, her long black hair was neatly tied back away from her face, her make-up appeared to be perfectly applied, and her eyeglasses were expensive and trendy. She obviously cared about her appearance, for she was slim and fit, but no matter what she did she was homely and tough-looking. Age lines were mapped across her white skin and no make-up could make her facial features smooth. I didn't know how old she was, but my guess would be in her mid-fifties. She never smiled, never seemed really to acknowledge my presence except to give me the distinct feeling that I was a bother rather than being viewed as a future asset. "Interesting," I thought to myself.

Minutes passed; audible pen scribbles could be heard as papers shuffled from the top of Cindy's desk to the "Out" box that sat in the upper right-hand corner of her desk. A tall, nondescript man came into Cindy's office without knocking. He had thin brown hair, cut military style; his face was clean-shaven. He didn't appear to wear glasses, and stooped slightly when he stood still. You could tell he didn't exercise much — or if he did it was at a gym, because his skin was pale white and he had a slight bulge around the belt line. However, he was very alert, for his brown eyes were evaluating me at the same time he was introducing himself. I assumed this must be the supervisor that Kelly had asked to come to her office. I automatically stood up as Rob Drake approached me with his hand extended, and we simultaneously said hello, followed by his welcome to the FAA and the LAX Field Office.

Finally, Cindy looked up from her paperwork and said, "Yes welcome. I am handing you off to Drake's care and he will get you processed in and show you who you will be working with and where your desk is. You will be working from 0730 to 1600 hours for the next three months while you are in training here. You will be assigned a work partner; his name is Special Agent Lee Stanton. Agent Stanton works for Rob Drake, who is our Supervisory Special Agent in Charge.

Supervisor Drake works directly for me. You got here today on time, but barely, so please plan accordingly and be here in the office, not the parking lot, at 0730. You are on probation for one year and can be released for being late to work." With that, she waved her hand in the air, dismissing both Drake and me from her office.

We both scrambled out quickly and I looked over at Drake, expecting some sort of explanation about her behavior, but not a word was said. I quietly followed him into his office and he pointed at the chair in front of his desk that he wanted me to be seated in. He then opened a folder and handed me several sheets of paper, explaining that I needed to fill each of them out completely in order to get a Los Angeles Airport Identification Badge, an employee parking permit, and an access control card to the office. He said once I had the paperwork complete he would introduce me to Agent Stanton, who would take me to the airport and make sure that all of my paperwork was submitted and processed today. Supervisor Drake further explained that Stanton would be my on-the-job training instructor for the next three months, so I was to follow his guidance and instructions to the letter. He would be training me in all facets of this job, from filling out my time card to conducting air carrier and airport inspections, checkpoint testing, opening investigative reports when regulatory discrepancies were found, and attending a variety of airport and air carrier meetings each month.

I completed the required paperwork. Drake took all of the papers from me and briefly scanned them, nodding and grinding his teeth slightly as he reviewed each page. With my paperwork in his hand he stood and motioned me to follow him out of his office and into the main area of the office — the "pit," as I learned it was fondly referred to. The very last desk in the back of the room near the makeshift kitchen was our destination, and it was where Agent Stanton was seated.

Well, I thought, *if the management team is this sullen, I wonder what Special Agent Stanton personality will reveal?* I walked slightly to the left of Drake, toward Agent Stanton's desk. There he was, sitting at his desk; his eyes had been following me across the room, eyes that were deep-set and glazed with suspicion, curiosity, and intrigue. I felt like he had looked into my brain, scanned it through and through, and then analyzed me inside and out, making a decision about me before I even got to his desk.

Supervisor Drake handed me off to Special Agent Lee Stanton without a word as he dropped my paperwork; it made a thump when it plopped on his desk. Agent Stanton stood up, looked at Drake, turned and looked at me and said, "Come on — let's get the hell outta here and go find a cup of coffee." He spoke with a distinctive deep calm voice that commanded attention and respect, along with a bit of fear. He was tall, well over 6'2," not slim, but fit in a bear-size of a man kind of way. I thought he epitomized the rugged mascu-line look of the famous John Wayne. He even had that swagger like John Wayne — always in control, always on the lookout, and always portraying a "don't mess with me" attitude. He was handsome in a cowboy way: big brown eyes, receding hairline, facial features that were rough, outdoor-attractive, and I immediately realized he was going to be one of the good guys. I could feel myself beginning to relax. Agent Stanton headed for the door with a brisk gait that set me off at a near run to keep up with him. As he passed the other agents in the office he stopped and introduced me briefly as his new partner, Special Agent Maggie Stewart. With that introduction, he sealed the deal; he was endeared to me already for treating me with the utmost respect on my first day of work. It was certainly more than I had re-ceived from the managers this morning. I was ready to work with my new partner, my confidence soaring.

We left the office, walking down the long flight of stairs and back outside into the California sunshine. We walked over to a set of cars parked in designated government parking spots, all looking exactly the same: same color black, same model, same everything. Agent Stanton began explaining the process for checking out a government car — or G-car, as they were referred to by government employees. Yes, they were all the same color, type, and model, so the only way you could figure out which car you were supposed to drive was to look at the license plate number and pick the one that matched the number on the set of keys you had checked out. That made sense to me. He had checked out a car when his shift started at 0600 in anticipation of my arrival, knowing we'd be going to the airport and the regional FAA office sometime during the day. The cars were all dirty, and Lee, as he asked me to call him from then on, had a pet peeve about this. He disliked dirty cars, and he further disliked the fact that most everyone in the office didn't want to take the time to have them cared for. It was one thing he would change and insist upon if he ever became a supervisor — that everyone would do their part to keep the G-cars clean and within all of the prescribed maintenance requirements.

"If you want to look professional, than everything about you needs to look professional, including the car you drive. Remember when you're a federal employee — aka 'fed' — everyone has their eye on you, everywhere you go. When you drive or walk around airports, airlines, cargo facilities, and even driving to lunch, you are being observed. So remember that." And he slapped me on the back with a firm whack.

We drove to the nearest coffee shop and ordered two cups of coffee, and proceeded to walk back to the G-car. "Let's go to the airport badging office first," said Lee, "and get your airport badge and schedule you for an air field training and driving test. To me this is the most important badge now — full airport access is critical if there is an emergency that the FAA needs to respond to. So let's go get this out of the way; plus there will be a line, so we'll have time to drink our coffees and get to know each other better."

When we arrived at the Los Angeles Airport Badging Office, located on Imperial Highway, we parked in a spot designated for G-cars and proceeded to walk into the badging office. Yes, indeed the line was long, and it snaked back and forth like the queue for a Disneyland ride. Agent Stanton told me to go stand in line and that he would be right back. I watch him saunter off with that cowboy gait of his, full of confidence and pride, and looking bigger than life. He walked up to the badging counter and said hello to the clerk; I could tell by her smile hat she recognized him, as she immediately picked up the telephone and made a call. After she had hung up the telephone, Agent Stanton smiled; I saw his lips say "Thank you, darling," and he turned and walked back toward me.

Within just a few seconds, a door opened and a man in a long-sleeved blue dress shirt with the LAX logo embroidered on the left chest pocket came out and greeted Agent Lee and me. Agent Stanton explained that I was new at the field office and needed an airport badge and to be scheduled for an airside training class. He asked me for my paperwork and said to wait there for a few minutes; then he turned and disappeared as quickly as he had come.

"Now, we wait," said Lee. "But it won't take too long, since we just cut the line big time. One perk of being a fed — but let me warn you, only do this when it's necessary, not just because you can. We have a great responsibility, especially after PSA 1771. Remember, everyone's eyes are on us, so be professional 24/7 from now on. So — why did you join the feds, and why are you here in LA?" Agent Stanton asked.

We chatted back and forth for about fifteen minutes about our personal lives. Agent Stanton was married with two children. His wife's name was Roberta and she was the vice president of an accounting firm. You could tell that his family was his pride and joy as he beamed showing his wide white teeth, which were in perfect alignment. Agent Stanton was six years older than I was, and had been with the FAA for eighteen months. He had retired from the US Marine Corps just months before getting hired with the FAA. He had graduated from the FAM class ahead of me and had flown five missions to date, mostly in Asia. The trips were three weeks at a stretch, so he had already logged many a mile in an airplane seat, and had spent several months away from home.

After being fingerprinted and having my picture taken, our wait was just minutes until my freshly printed badge was placed in my hands and I was given a slip of paper with a date and time to return for my airside driving training and exam. Agent Stanton called this SIDA Training, which meant Security Identification Display Area. He informed me that I would get all of the necessary training back at the office and in a video presentation that the airport showed when I went back. He let me know in no uncertain terms that I would be well-prepared in time for my driving and written examination. "There's nothing like driving along B-747s with the smell of jet fuel filling up your nose," he said with a wink and a smile.

Back in the G-car, we drove to the FAA Regional Office, where once again I had my picture and fingerprints taken, and a freshly printed and still slightly warm badge was placed in my hands. , *YES, I am officially part of the team now,* I thought, and I was so proud.

We spoke with the regional director, Ed Smith; the deputy director, Thomas Bean; and several of the staff people, along with the division secretary, Tina, before leaving the building. Director Smith apologized to me for not attending my FAM graduation, but he had other matters here that needed his attention at the last minute and he was not able to fly out to Arizona to attend the graduation. I nodded that I understood, and said I appreciated that he thought of our class. Agent Stanton explained that the regional staff wrote policies, etc. supporting all of the field efforts that were handled at the field offices. There were field offices in Hawaii, Arizona, Nevada, and California, and the staff here supported all of those offices. In his opinion, it wasn't as much fun as field work, but it was a necessary cog in the civil aviation security wheel.

All of my paperwork was gone, which meant that Agent Stanton and I had accomplished everything we needed to do outside of the field office. "Before we go back to the office, let's grab a bite to eat. I never pack a lunch, and I'm hungry," Agent Stanton said. That was all right with me; it was only 10:45 a.m., but I was hungry too. Agent Stanton didn't ask or say where we were going. I was beginning to figure out in short order that Lee just "did," and he didn't ask permission much, if at all.

We stopped at a hole-in-the-wall Mexican restaurant. As we sat down on the open-air patio, the server, who knew Lee by his first name, brought chips and salsa to the table. "I know what you're having," the server said to Agent Stanton, "but what will the lady be having?" I quickly ordered two shredded beef tacos with rice and beans, and then dove into the warm salty chips and thick red salsa, for I was suddenly famished. Agent Stanton's order turned out to be two beef enchiladas with rice and beans. We each had a Coke.

When we got back to the office, Agent Stanton handed me a thick binder that was called an ACSSP, Air Carrier Standard Security Program. "This is similar to what you saw and learned about in FAM training, but as you know, there will be another school you will have to attend for airport and air carrier security training. But until those classes are available, start reading this ACSSP. For the next few months, until you go to Oklahoma City (OKC) later this year for four weeks of training, you'll be conducting stealth checkpoint testing with me, and going with me to the airports I have responsibility for and the associated airlines and cargo facilities at those airports. It's a lot to learn, but the more you can learn here before going to training, the easier it will be for you in OKC. So take all of this stuff to your desk and start reading for the next couple of hours. I have a few things to do, but I'll see you before the end of the day. Got any questions?"

"Nope," I said. "Thanks, Agent Stanton — see you later." I walked to my desk, put everything down, adjusted my chair after sitting in it a couple of times, and cracked the ACSSP for an insight into the world of aviation security.

At 1500 hours, Agent Stanton came and sat down in the chair beside my desk. The desk and chairs were almost as worn as the carpet, but they were sturdy government furniture. Lee explained that our office was going to be relocated next year to a brand new building on Century Boulevard. The pluses of the move were new offices and equipment, but the negatives were that we were going to be off-airport so we'd have to drive just a little farther to get back and forth to the LAX Airport Management and our air carriers. But it wasn't our call, so no sense worrying about it. He also told me that he had spoken to Supervisor Drake about my work hours and had gotten permission for me to switch to coming into work at 0600 versus 0730. I was elated, for this would align me with Agent Stanton's hours, definitely make the commute easier, and give me time after work to go for a run and eventually find a place to live. We talked until 1600 hours about what I had read so far in the ACSSP, and Agent Stanton provided me with answers to my questions and clarification of things I had barely thought about. *This guy is one smart dude*, I thought; *I lucked out to have him as a partner.*

While walking to my car, I ran into Big Earl. We greeted each other by way of hugs, and briefly chatted about our day. He had a fifty-mile commute one way back and forth to work every day, and he hadn't been authorized yet to work the earlier shift. He said he liked his trainer/partner just fine and asked how I liked mine. He asked the question with a serious look and tone — why, I wasn't quite sure, but I told Big Earl I was really fortunate to have Lee Stanton as my trainer/partner. Big Earl replied, "Really? His nickname is 'The Duke' — you know, because he looks like John Wayne, and everyone says he is one tough and sometimes mean SOB."

"Good to know," I said, "but so far he's been great. Very informative, and he sure knows how to cut through the red tape. See you tomorrow, Earl — drive safe."

"Will do," he said, and we turned and walked to our cars.

The drive home was worse than the drive in. It was hard to imagine that it took forty-five minutes to drive five miles. Welcome to southern California — and remember to live close to the office, Maggie. By the time I parked my car and got my running gear on, it was almost dark — another reminder that starting work at 0600 was going to be a blessing.

I ran along The Strand at the beach again. I ran the same path, the identical three glorious miles in the fading sunlight with seagulls above looking for sanctuary for the evening, and people seeking the same as they ducked into their homes, hotels, or nearby restaurants for a bite to eat. The crashing of the waves on the beach reminded me that the ocean was near and ever-present. It was a perfect way to end my day.

I needed my Sandhill Crane alarm to wake me up for my second day of work. 0415 did not come naturally to me, so the alarm was a welcome sound so early in the morning. No sunrise from the east, no birds squawking or chirping, no tires squealing in the parking lot below, just the ever-present sound of the ocean, reminding me that life was grand. I got up again to the chilly beach air and immediately turned on the coffee pot as I began getting ready for my day.

I left my room at 0525 so I would have plenty of time to get to the office. The traffic was heavier than I anticipated for that time of the morning, but I made it to the office in fifteen minutes, was granted immediate access to the government parking lot, thanks to my new FAA identification badge, and quickly climbed the stairs, arriving at the office with ten minutes to spare. "Okay, Maggie, that was perfect." As I opened the main office door, there stood Special Agent Lee Stanton with a cup of coffee in one hand, and one eye on his wrist watch, and one on me as I walked in the door. *I should have known he'd beat me here,* I said to myself. *I'll have to work on that!* Agent Stanton smiled and said, "Grab a cup of coffee and let's go. We're heading to the airport to do some checkpoint testing."

I grabbed a cup of coffee, and off we went. Agent Stanton threw me the G-car keys and said, "You drive. We're cutting across the air field to the terminals, and it's time for some airside on-the-job training."

We accessed the airside of the airport from the security gate located directly beside our field office. The security guard on duty looked at both Stanton's and my airport access IDs, ensured that the G-car had the proper decals and sticker to be allowed airside. We did, and as we passed, Lee told the guard to be sure and not call ahead that we were coming. "Listen up," he said to the guard with a stern look, "Air Operations doesn't need to be calling anyone that we're out and about. Understand? I don't want to have to come back here and speak to you or your supervisor after we get spotted." The guard nodded in affirmation, along with a worried look on his face that he understood.

"What was that all about I asked?" Agent Stanton said that sometimes the gate guards would call ahead and reveal our testing schedule when they saw us access these gates. "It's hard enough now to get any valid testing done since our cadre is so small here, so we are pretty easily identified — and remember what I said yesterday about always being observed. Well, sometimes that happens too much, and for covert checkpoint testing, being identified ahead of time is a bad thing."

We pulled away from the guard post, and Agent Stanton began asking me what speed I was required to drive on at the taxiways and what some of the rules of the airport roads were. "Fifteen miles an hour — and never cross an active runway without permission from the air traffic controller working the ground control on frequency 121.65 or 121.75 depending if your at the north or south complex at LAX," I said. "Always look out for the larger aircraft to ensure that their wing span doesn't overlap the taxiway you are driving on, and be aware of the catering trucks and baggage tugs for falling debris. Debris or foreign object damage (FOD) is very dangerous at airports because the debris can get sucked up into an aircraft engine, causing severe damage to the aircraft when it's still on the ground or even deadlier consequences if the aircraft gets airborne. Finally, never drive behind the aft or back side of an aircraft because your vehicle can get blown over by the aircrafts jet blast. Okay," I said. "I forgot how you tell if an aircraft is running or not or just sitting on a taxiway, or if they are shut down and waiting for some type of air traffic clearance. I remember the obvious if you can't hear them, but there's something else. What did I miss?" I asked Stanton.

Agent Stanton turned and smiled at me, saying that he was extremely proud of me that I asked questions when I did not understand or remember something. In this profession, especially one that is full of male egos, it was always best to ask questions and seek explanations. "In regard to determining if an aircraft is running or not, look for the landing lights, all of them: port, starboard, and aft. If they are running and an aircraft is out on the airfield somewhere, then the aircraft engines are on. So the best advice I can give you is not to drive behind any aircraft unless it is absolutely necessary. Now let's drive on over to Terminal One, and let's do some checkpoint testing."

As I approached the intersection to turn onto the taxiway and begin my drive toward the terminal of LAX various airlines, food service and maintenance trucks sped past me, sensing that I was the newbie on the airfield that day. And every driver was probably chuckling as they drove past and saw the complete look of concentration on my face, knowing that I was a federal agent, since we had just placed big blue placards on each side of our vehicle saying "FAA Official" prior to being allowed access onto the airfield. Agent Stanton didn't say one word; he just looked straight ahead. I could see him out of the corner of my eye with his aviation sunglasses disguising what movement his eyes were really tracking, and I had no clue what he was thinking. When we got near the Tom Bradley International, I stopped short of the intersecting taxiway and waited. A China Airlines B-747 was just approaching the intersection, and I had heard on the radio that they had been given clearance to taxi to the departing runway via the taxiway we were on. So we needed to sit tight and let them taxi past us and turn toward their departure runway. As she passed, with her tail reaching into the blue sky, the equivalent of a six-story-tall building, I looked up at the portals and saw the tiny faces of the passengers nestled inside this gigantic white painted bird, some looking anxious, some excited, and some bored already, as the aircraft taxied and they readied themselves for their long flight to some exotic foreign destination. As the eighteen tires passed, four under each wing, eight on the under carriage, and two at the nose gear, I felt as if I had shrunk in size and became miniature, for those Goodrich 260-pound black tires, rolling past us, dwarfed our vehicle. It was surreal. I heard nothing but jet engines, and smelled the fumes of aviation gasoline, as the aircraft passed us, moving farther and farther into the long line of other aircraft, waiting for their take-off clearances.

Agent Stanton poked me in the shoulder and I looked over at him as he pointed for us to drive to the right, toward the terminal area and away from the taxiway. We were rampside now, and we could drive from here to Terminal One without getting in too many aircraft paths.

When we arrived at Terminal One, we parked the G-car underneath the terminal. Agent Lee said that we were not going to put our airport badges on because he wanted to see if we could walk from the vehicle and up the outside stairs and into the terminal area to see if any of the airline employees working on the ramp would challenge us by asking us who we were and ask for our identification. It was a federal requirement that every employee working at an airport wear a valid identification badge issued by that airport. And today Agent Stanton did not want us to wear ours. "Okay by me," I said. So I kept my airline ID tucked beneath my white dress shirt, and my badge in my jacket pocket.

We opened and closed our car doors at the same time, and I immediately could hear the rattling of baggage conveyor belts underneath the terminal just a few feet away from us. I could see the many colors of bags swirling around in every direction as they moved in this massive baggage system, either to reach their airplane on time or to get back to their owner. It was hard to imagine that this massive, confusing-looking system of belts, metal, and hinges could get any bag to its proper destination.

Agent Stanton and I moved toward the flight of stairs to the terminal, and we passed two employees who nodded at us, but did not challenge who we were or why we were there. So we proceeded up the stairs and opened a door that placed us in the jetway bridge. Agent Stanton had me write down the date, time, and number of the jet bridge we had entered. He also said to write down Martinez and Schaffer. To our left was the exit to the terminal and to our right was a B-737 aircraft. We turned and walked toward the open cabin door of the B-737. When we entered the aircraft, there was a cleaning crew on board who barely raised their heads vs. acknowledging our existence. We both walked into the cockpit and Agent Stanton told me to get a business card out of my credential wallet. We placed both of our business cards on the left seat — the captain's seat in the cockpit. When we turned to leave, we waved at the cleaning crew and then proceeded up the jet bridge and into the terminal.

Once we were in the terminal, he turned to me and again gave me instructions as to what to record in the small notebook that I had pulled from my jacket pocket earlier. Agent Stanton had me record the tail number of the aircraft, which we could now see from inside the terminal as we looked out the terminal window. And he said the Martinez and Shaffer were the two employees we had passed on the ramp. He noted their names as we walked past them. "When you go to an airline to discuss the breaches in security that we just witnessed, the first thing they are going to ask for is the names of the employees that you passed while walking on the ramp. And if you can't give them dates, times, locations, and names, you will have no credibility," Agent Stanton said.

"I think our identities will be discovered soon," he went on. "So, let's go conduct one more checkpoint test; then we'll let the airline know that we are here and what happened."

Agent Stanton asked me to take the test piece, an encapsulated small firearm, and place it in my jacket pocket. Once the test piece was in my jacket, we proceeded to the security checkpoint and got in line. I felt nervous, almost like I was doing something wrong. I had always been a law-abiding citizen, so it felt very out of character to attempt to break the law. Agent Stanton and I presented our credentials to the security agent and proceeded on through to the carry-on screening process. Agent Stanton dropped back a few passengers behind me, and I was left on my own to conduct the test. I removed my shoes and placed them in one bin and placed my jacket in the second bin. Before and behind me, other passengers were doing the same rote exercise, never suspecting who I was or what I was doing.

I smiled at the screeners as I passed through the walk-through metal detector without any alarms indicating my intent to do harm. And as quickly as I had placed my shoes and jacket on the belt for the x-ray machine, they were returned to me. I picked up my jacket in my left hand and my shoes in my right and moved several feet away from the x-ray machine, turned, and waited for Agent Lee to clear the screening process.

Once he was clear, he motioned me to walk with him over to the supervisor's podium at the checkpoint. We identified ourselves, cell phones were used to call management, screeners were pulled from various positions, and the debriefing madness began.

Several hours later, Agent Stanton and I returned to the office and advised our supervisor of what had occurred. I was shown how to pull an official Enforcement Investigation Report (EIR) number for the report that would be written against the airlines in the next thirty days.

My first day of checkpoint testing was one of many over the next several months. Some tests were successful, in that the screeners found the test piece we had hidden in various bags or on our person, and others sailed through the screening equipment as easily as a $300K racing yacht sails to Catalina in the choppy waters found between the shores of California and the tiny island. I didn't like the failures for two reasons: one, it was a vulnerability to the traveling public; and two, someone always lost their job. Jobs were hard to come by in this tough economy; but in reality, those test pieces should have been detected. The bags we presented to the screening checkpoints did not contain nearly the amount of items that a regular passenger carried in their bags, so in my opinion, the items should have been detected.

I studied airport manuals, security programs, airline security recommendations, and walked the ramps, terminals, baggage make-up areas and street-side areas of each terminal at LAX. I studied and worked daily with Agent Stanton before Supervisor Drake notified me that my "official" training class in Oklahoma City (OKC) had been scheduled to begin the second week in October.

With his next breath, Drake very casually said, "You've also been scheduled for your first air marshal mission, and you're leaving this coming Sunday for a three-week trip to Asia."

Agent Stanton shook my hand, and gave me a hug and a pat on the back on the way out the door. "See Kelly in the morning — she has your flight and hotel information for Seattle. You'll make me proud. I know it," he said with a smile. "I'll see you in the morning."

I had rented a small apartment a block from the beach. The city of Redondo Beach surrounded the coastal city of Hermosa Beach, where I had rented a hotel room for a month. I knew it was time to move into a less expensive place to live, so I went looking for an apartment. As I got to know the area better, by zig- zagging in and out of Hermosa Beach, Redondo Beach, and Manhattan Beach, I soon discovered the Riviera, an area in Redondo nestled just a few blocks from the beach that was rich with apartments, restaurants, and specialty shops. It was expensive, but when I found the small one-bedroom beach cottage with a garage and a washer and dryer all to myself, I couldn't resist. The small street of Camino De La Costa, one block from the beach — and just a few blocks from everything else I could ever need — was perfect for the outdoor lover and walker that I was.

I knew for the first year I was going to have a very tight budget, since I was starting out with the FAA as a GS-7 (General Scale). Because my job was in a technical category, each year I would advance a pay grade until I reached a GS-12. After that, I would have to start applying for other positions to advance into management, but I didn't have to think about that for several years. My immediate goal was to be the best damn agent I could be, pass all of my required training, and work hard to protect my fellow travelers.

I didn't have any plants or pets yet, so I could basically put my mail on hold, close the front door to my apartment, and travel as I needed with very few, if any worries. My life was simple and easy, and I was having the adventure of a lifetime. I felt at the top of my game, confident in my abilities, confident in my confidence, and knowing I was making a difference in the world. It was exhilarating.

I was looking forward to going for additional training, and then on my first mission, as I literally danced out the door, while dashing off for a run to quell the excitement that was running wildly through my veins. Finally, five months after graduating from FAM Training, I was scheduled for a mission.

CHAPTER FOUR

The Wait is Over

THE NEXT MORNING when I arrived at the office, I saw Big Earl smiling, too — well, if you could call it a smile. He was an enormous guy who looked scary as hell and had a voice to match his physical appearance, and he didn't smile. He looked and acted like a cop one hundred percent of the time. He was retired from the Air Force special police, and had the attitude of "I've seen it all, and if you get the attention of the police, it's usually for a reason," so a lot of people steered away from him. Not me — I fortunately had gotten to know him during our FAM basic training, so I knew he was really a kitty cat underneath that rough and gruff exterior of his. But I'd never tell him that!

We both headed for the coffee pot at the same time, to refill our empty cups, and we began talking about our upcoming first mission. Big Earl knew the air marshal coordinator in Washington, DC, and knew we would be going to Asia for three weeks to support the Seoul Summer Olympics beginning September 17th through the 2nd of October. Big Earl said that teams had been flying in and out of Seoul, South Korea, for months, in preparation for the two-week event. We wouldn't have much ground time, just lots of time flying around Asia.

Big Earl said that Drake had told him there would be a conference call today that would provide us more information, around 10:00 a.m. Kelly, the administrative assistant for the office, was arranging our airline flights to Seattle, WA, where the team would originate. The rest of the ticketing, logistics, and other details, were handled by the FAM coordinator in Washington, DC.

Just a few minutes before 10:00 a.m., Big Earl and I went into the conference room to dial into the meeting. A few minutes earlier, Kelly had brought me a piece of paper with a telephone number and password we needed to use. It was 10:00 a.m. Pacific Standard Time and 1:00 p.m. in Washington, DC.

I dialed the number, punched in the password as instructed, and put the telephone on speaker mode so Big Earl and I could both hear the ongoing conversation. An automated voice stated that the password had been accepted, and to wait to be connected to the conference. Kelly, who had been standing at the conference room doorway, making sure we dialed in correctly, turned and quietly left once she had heard that we were connected properly.

After a few minutes of various clicks, rings, and static, voices began permeating the telephone line of the conference call. The FAM coordinator spoke up, and began calling names. After everyone was identified, he advised us that this conversation was being conducted on an unsecure line, and that the essential details of the actual mission itself would be given to us in an in-person briefing after our arrival in Seattle next week. The purpose of this conference call was only to make sure everyone knew the dates of the trip, the hotel to stay at in Seattle, and the time for our first meeting once we all arrived.

Everyone was advised to travel this coming Sunday from their duty stations. It didn't matter what time they arrived in Seattle, as long as they were at the scheduled meeting that began at 0800 hours on Monday morning. All briefings, documents, and equipment checks would take place on Monday. The trip destinations, and obvious purpose, everyone already knew, but all additional trip details would be given out when the team assembled in Seattle. The FAM coordinator asked if everyone had their flights booked. He asked again by calling out each agent's name to affirm that they did. Everyone responded that their flight reservations were made. Again, he told us the name of our hotel and that our team leader had been identified, but that name was not provided during this conference call either. Thirty minutes later, Big Earl and I hung up the conference room telephone, disconnecting the line with a swift touch of one button, turned off the lights, closed the door, and went back to our desks.

At the end of the day, I looked for Agent Stanton, but I couldn't find him, so instead I left him a note on his desk. I waved good night to Kelly, and left the office for the day — well, actually for the next three weeks, thinking of everything I needed to do between this afternoon and Sunday afternoon, when I departed on Alaska Airlines for Seattle.

I spent part of my afternoon getting a short run in at the beach. This time I ran along the shore's edge, getting my shoes wet in the cool but refreshing ocean. Along the way I even stopped, picking up a couple of smooth, worn sea glass pieces for my growing collection at home. This run would be the one luxury of the weekend, for I had tons and tons of stuff to do, and the clock was ticking.

I pulled out my large yellow hard-sided Samsonite suitcase that I had purchased specifically for these types of trips. Every FAM needed this type of suitcase to transport their firearm in when they weren't on official duty. The trip from Los Angeles to Seattle would not be an official air marshal flight for me. I was flying to position for a mission, so my gun had to be transported in my hard-sided suitcase. Federal regulations required that I have my firearm unloaded, and locked in this type of suitcase.

I had found this suitcase a few months ago while I was shopping up at the Peninsula Center Shopping Mall in Rolling Hills Estates. I loved this little shopping center because it was all outdoors, with plenty of shops, eateries, and a first-class movie theater that never seemed crowded. The luggage store was family-owned, the staff there was very personable, and their prices were competitive with other stores in the area. While I was window shopping one day, waiting for my movie time to get closer, I spied the yellow suitcase standing just inside the store. I immediately knew that I was going to buy it. It was perfect for what I needed: hard-sided, lockable, and it was bright yellow, which would make it easy to spot on any luggage carousel regardless of what country I was in. I quickly entered the store, retrieved my prize, paid for it with my FAA Federal Credit Union VISA credit card, and headed back toward my Jeep, placing the suitcase in the back, before walking back to the movies.

At home, I packed, unpacked, and packed again. I hadn't been on travel for three weeks in a very long time, so I vacillated back and forth on what to take. The weather would be good in Asia this time of year, which made packing easier than having to pack bulky winter clothes. After I packed the second time, or third time, I don't remember, I finally snapped my suitcase closed, and stood it upright. *You could drive yourself crazy packing, Maggie Stewart,* I thought as I rolled it into the living room.

I spent the rest of Saturday stopping my mail, letting my landlord know that I would be on extended travel, making cab arrangements for the following day, and making sure once again that I had my flight information and passport.

Then I settled down to an early dinner, feeling confident that I was prepared and ready. Gosh, the excitement was almost unbearable.

When I arrived at the airport, I needed to go to a ticket agent and check in because I had a firearm with me and I needed to declare that it was in checked baggage, unloaded, and with no accessible ammunition. At the ticket counter I presented my airline flight information, my air marshal credentials, and a smile. The ticket agent reviewed everything in detail and began clicking away on her keyboard, which was hidden from my view, only to be seen by the agent who was madly typing, her acrylic nails making a tap, tap, tap on the keyboard with each stroke. She prepared a bag tag for my beloved yellow suitcase and asked if I had anything else that needed to be checked or declared. I said no, and she then circled what gate my flight was departing from and motioned to the right, indicating where screening was, and the departure gate.

As I headed toward the gate I heard the plop of my luggage as it was added to the busy conveyor belt that disappeared deep into the airport as bags were whisked away to their destination. Well — that's what everyone hoped for, at least. I had never lost a checked bag yet, and I was hoping that this wouldn't be a first. I didn't like leaving my firearm behind, but because this was a non-working flight segment for me, I had no choice. So off I walked with a slight bit of attitude in my gait, I was sure, toward the checkpoint.

Again, screening was efficient and quick. I sometimes wondered, now that I was an agent, if the efficiency was due to inattentiveness versus skill. I had been a direct witness, and had already begun writing civil penalty cases against airlines for their failure — or their contract screening company's failure — to adequately screen the passengers that were passing through their checkpoints. Checkpoint screening was critical to the aviation security infrastructure, and I wondered why it was handled by contractors and not either directly by the airport or the airlines themselves. No one was ever really able to give me a satisfactory answer to that question when I asked.

I boarded the Alaska Airlines flight for the two-hour flight to Seattle, found my aisle seat, and took out my book to continue reading where I had left off. Even though I was not officially working on this flight, I always kept an eye open, scanning the aircraft's interior and its passengers from time to time to see what was going on. I listened and watched as I was trained to do. No firearm, but we had learned other tactical skills in our FAM training, so I was confident I could assist the flight crew if I were ever needed.

Agent Stanton had told me that there was a new violation program called "Interference with Crew Member," in that individuals that interfered with the safety of the aircraft or its crew could be fined, or put in jail if criminal charges were filed. The FAA Flight Standards Division was taking the lead for this regulatory program, since they were the organization within the FAA that oversaw the pilot and flight attendant regulatory programs. I asked why FAA Security didn't oversee these types of incidents, since it seemed more like a security issue than a safety issue. Agent Stanton didn't answer; I suspected he had an opinion, but he wasn't willing to voice his opinion … at least not right then.

So for now, I buckled my seatbelt, and let my book sit idle in my lap until everyone had gotten on board and was seated. When I heard the cabin bell chime, indicating that the forward door had been closed, I knew it wouldn't be long before we left the gate and began our journey toward Seattle.

After we landed, I found my way to baggage claim and was extremely pleased to see that big yellow suitcase coming off the baggage belt as it was unceremoniously spit out onto the carousel with other bags tumbling around it. I saw firsthand why it was so important to have a hard-sided suitcase for this type of travel.

I hopped the hotel shuttle for the short ride to the hotel, got checked in, dropped my bag in my room, changed into my running clothes, and headed back downstairs for a run. In cities that I didn't know, I traditionally had gotten into the habit of running near the hotel unless I was with someone who knew the area. It made sense, to me at least, that getting lost, or getting caught in bad weather wasn't the smartest thing to do. I always took a twenty-dollar bill, too.

I stopped at the front desk, grabbed a bottle of complimentary water, and headed for the lobby doors. I passed a small dining area adjacent to the hotel lobby, so I knew I wouldn't have to go out to find dinner later.

People say it always rains a lot in Seattle, but on this glorious Sunday afternoon the skies were clear and it was in the low 70s. My run was slightly boring, yet refreshing, as I ran around the various hotels that were clustered together on the mile-long block. As I always do, I was looking for dropped coins along the way. I loved finding money, any amount, any condition; rough from tires trying to smash them into the asphalt, or freshly dropped, still shiny and new, I would pick them up regardless of their condition and place them in my pocket. Alas, today I didn't find any. At home I had a special jar that I put my running money in; I would save it so I could see how much I'd found at the end of the year.

When I got back to the hotel, Big Earl was just checking in. He was talking to someone else in line, so I assumed he was another team member. I walked up; Earl and I hugged, and I turned and extended my hand to the gentleman and said, "Hello, I'm Maggie Stewart." We shook hands and he said his name was George Masters and he was the team leader for this trip. We all agreed to meet for dinner downstairs in about an hour. With that said, I headed for my room to change and get the clothes out that I was going to wear tomorrow morning.

After dinner, it was early lights out, for I was tired from the previous weeks of long hours, and the rush of getting ready for this trip. I just wanted to sleep so the wait would be over, and I'd be one day closer to flying my first mission.

At 0800 hours the next morning, everyone had gathered in a small conference room on the mezzanine floor of the hotel called the Swan Room. Its seating capacity looked to be suited for about twenty-five people, with long conference tables standing in neat rows waiting for any guests to occupy the chairs pushed under each table. There were no pictures, just dull tan paint. The paint looked new, but still dull. I went and sat down by Big Earl just as the meeting was about to begin.

Agent Masters introduced himself and asked that everyone please call him by his first name, George. He was a very tall man; six foot five would be my guess, with an average build, brown hair, and brown eyes that were partially hidden by extremely thick glasses. His ears were slightly out of proportion compared to his head size, as they stuck out a little; his nose was straight, and his lips were average. He wasn't handsome, but he wasn't homely, either; average-looking except for his height.

I looked around and saw that I was the only female on this team, and I silently wondered where Colleen or Georgia was. It would have been nice to be flying with either one of them on our first mission.

George had everyone introduce themselves and say what field office they were based out of. Once the introductions were complete, George immediately got down to business, explaining various aspects of the mission. Some parts of this discussion were sensitive and others were logistical. Everyone listened intently, and not a word was spoken except by George.

We would be flying at 1500 hours tomorrow from Seattle to Narita, Japan. Over the next three weeks we would be in and out of Narita, Japan; Seoul, South Korea; Manila, Philippines; Bangkok, Thailand; Hong Kong, and Singapore. He said we would not be in-country very long at any of these locations because the purpose of our mission was to continuously fly on US air carriers that were operating from those locations, specifically flying passengers to and from the Olympic venue in Seoul.

We would have some down time in these countries, but usually less than twenty-four hours. When we were on the ground our free time was ours, except for scheduled team meetings.

George went through all of the state department rules of etiquette that we were mandated to follow, along with various safety recommendations and places, if any, that we were restricted from visiting.

We were given all of our hotel and flight information in neat packets and told to guard these with our lives!

The meeting lasted about two hours before we were dismissed for the morning. We would be meeting again at a different location later that afternoon to go through a weapon, ammunition, and gear check.

At the end of our scheduled meeting in the afternoon, George again reminded us that the team would be departing the next day at 1500 hours for Narita, Japan. We needed to be in the hotel lobby, checked out of our rooms, and ready to go to the airport by 1100 hours sharp.

The following morning I had checked out of my room and was ready to go. In fact, I was so excited that I was the first one in the lobby at 1030. I got to see each team member meander in one by one. We all jammed into the hotel courtesy shuttle van for the 35-minute ride to the airport. We talked some, but mainly stared out the window as we passed the green tree-lined lakes that dotted this beautiful city.

International travel was completely different in every aspect of the check-in process. You had to be at the airport an additional three hours before flight time. There was additional scrutiny, even prior to actually getting to the ticket counter, where you would present your ticket information and your passport. This segment of the flight process for us was no different than for any other passenger traveling to Narita later that afternoon. We all endured the wait in line, moving our bags an inch at a time as each passenger finally made it to the front of the line, to be waved over to the ticket counter by an airline agent for check-in. I was glad to be able to place my carry-on bag on top of my big yellow suitcase as we moved at a snail's pace through the line. My carry-on was pretty heavy because I had quickly stuffed three or four paperback books into it when I learned that the flight from Seattle to Narita was nine hours and thirty-two minutes. At the airport as everyone got themselves organized, I quickly grabbed some best sellers off the closest bookstore rack. "Bring books with you from now on, Maggie," I quietly whispered under my breath as I walked back to the team.

It took well over an hour for everyone to get checked in, watch their luggage get screened and loaded on a cart, and then placed on the baggage belt behind the ticket counter by a guy who looked like he should have been a professional football player and not a "bag rat" working at the airport. This guy was gigantic, with hands the size of melons, and a scowl on his face that clearly said "Don't mess with me."

The station manager on duty for our airline met us near the end of the ticket counter and asked all of us to follow her. It was her responsibility to get us beyond the screening checkpoint and introduce us to the captain and first officer for the flight. We quickly and quietly stepped behind the ticket counter and disappeared through an unmarked door that led us into the operations area. We passed lockers, a tiny break room, and several offices stuffed with people, music blasting, and other noises filling the air as they read various computer screens and pieces of paper, while readying themselves to get our flight and other flights safely into the skies over Seattle.

Behind the scenes at an airport is entirely different. The beauty that is presented in airline terminals is certainly not found here. The floors are scuffed, dirty, and worn from airline employees moving back and forth across them twenty-four hours a day, seven days a week, and three hundred sixty-five days a year. The furniture looks worn and tired from never getting a break. The walls are patched with almost the same shades of paint, but not quite. Yet this place was very much alive, steaming with rich accents, shapes, and colors of every type of human being imaginable. The only sameness was the color of their uniforms. It was like this dusty inner city had brought together the world for one common purpose: the purpose of aviation. You could see that everyone we passed had a love, an admiration, a thrill for being in the jobs they were in. It was their passion and their focus, and I was very happy to be amongst these flyers.

The station manager bid us farewell as she introduced George, our team leader, to the captain. The first officer was outside doing a pre-flight walk-around check of the B-747 that we would be flying on today, so we would meet him later. The captain turned and said hello to all of us, and stated that he was very happy to have us aboard. He gave us a weather briefing and the flight time to Narita, and advised us that he would notify the chief flight attendant that we were on board, and would ask her to bring him all of our seat assignments. Federal regulations required the flight crew to know the seat assignments for any armed passenger. The captain advised George that if any other authorized individuals were onboard, that he would get word to him where they were seated.

We proceeded to board prior to the passengers, and sat in our designated seats. I was in the economy section. I put my backpack under the seat in front of me, and pushed it all the way forward and to the left. That way I'd have some room to stretch out my feet now and again. I stuffed one of the paperback books I had purchased in the seat pocket in front of me and I began watching people as they boarded, struggling to get their luggage stuffed into the overhead bins and then crawling over people to get into their seats, especially in the center rows of this aircraft, which were five seats across.

I felt my mind shift as I began looking at people differently as they maneuvered themselves into their seats. Good guy, bad guy, who to watch and who to assume might be okay. "Never assume anything, Maggie," I reminded myself, but profiling at some point had to be done so you wouldn't put your mind into complete sensory overload.

The flight attendants performed the security briefings in English and Japanese, so the briefing lasted longer than those given on domestic flights, and I could tell that we were taxiing at a slower rate of speed so the crew had plenty of time to finish their briefing, along with making sure everyone's seat backs were in the upright position, carry-on luggage stowed beneath their seats, and seatbelts fastened. Once they were seated in the back, middle, and forward sections of the aircraft, I knew we were just about ready to depart.

The nine and a half hour flight was long, tiring, and uneventful. Fortunately, I didn't have anyone seated next to me, so I had a little more room to flex my arms and lean toward the seat next to mine. We did not sleep and we did not get up from our seats unless we needed to go to the lavatory. Staying in position was critical. We were served dinner, followed by an evening snack before the cabin lights were turned off, and breakfast before we landed. The food had the typical cardboard flavor and a texture that I could not describe, especially the eggs at breakfast. But I was hungry, so I ate every single bite of food that was placed before me.

When we landed in Narita, we deplaned with the rest of the passengers and proceeded toward the customs stations. George had instructed us to meet him before we cleared customs, so I was the last one to arrive since I was the marshal at the back of the aircraft.

Everyone looked tired but alert. The first leg of our three-week journey had been uneventful, which was exactly what we wanted. The team leader checked in with the local law enforcement at the airport and followed the established protocol that was required of us as armed guests of their country. An hour later we left the airport, with our luggage in tow, taking taxis to the Radisson Hotel, which was a fifteen-minute ride from the airport.

As we left the airport I saw immediately that perimeter security was much tighter here than in any airport in the United States. Double gates and guards with large machine guns separated us from the lush countryside that awaited us just outside the fence line. I saw that all vehicles were stopped and inspected, and the drivers were required to present their airport identification badges both before entering and exiting the airport. This was a much more onerous security system than we had in place in America.

We barely had twelve hours on the ground before we would be flying again. I calculated that by the time we checked in, conducted our team debriefing, and met three and half hours before departure tomorrow morning to Seoul, we'd have just enough time to eat and maybe get about five hours of sleep.

The Radisson Hotel was your typical-looking high-rise American-style hotel. The lobby was modern with on-site dining, a business center, indoor and outdoor swimming pool, and two saunas. After checking in and receiving my room key, I asked about places to run and was told that the hotel was very close to the Sakura-no-Yama Hill and Naritasan Shinshoji Temple. I could follow a small road from the hotel along rice paddies to the temple and back. I was given a small map that showed the route for the run; it was approximately four miles, round trip. What an ingenious idea to be given a map that you could carry with you on a run. I had never seen this anywhere else, and I made a mental note to keep this map, since it was such a great idea. No one else on the team would go with me, so I decided to go alone. The route looked pretty straightforward, so I felt confident I would be fine and not get myself lost.

The room was tiny, and the bathroom even tinier, and I wondered how some of our team members were going to fit into the small bath-tub, for I could see that I would barely fit, having to bend my knees and curl my legs up. But having a private bathroom was wonderful.

Our team met and George led us through the debrief, collecting the information he needed to send back to Washington, DC. The meeting lasted about forty-five minutes. Several of the team members decided to walk into town and have dinner, but since I needed a run first I told them I'd probably have room service tonight. George wrapped the meeting up and advised everyone to be in the lobby at 0530 hours tomorrow morning. Our flight from Narita to Seoul was departing at 0930.

Blurry-eyed at 0530 the following morning, the team assembled in the lobby for the short shuttle ride to the airport. This trip pattern was identical to the previous day's, but in reverse. Upon arrival at the airport we checked in with local law enforcement, then the ticket counter, customs, screening, and boarded the aircraft. I was seated in economy again, but today the flight from Narita to Seoul was only one hour and thirty minutes. The flight was completely booked and everyone seemed as tired as we were, since it was so early in the morning.

When we arrived in Seoul, the process for departing the aircraft, going through customs, and meeting local law enforcement was very similar to the process that we followed in Narita. However, the law enforcement officials here were intrigued that a woman was a federal agent, much less an air marshal. They kept asking George questions, and then staring at me. I instinctively knew they were talking about me, and I continued to eye them through my aviator sunglasses, looking away only when it was apparent that George had finally convinced them that I was part of the team. "I'll explain later," George said to me. "Let's get out of here."

This flight too had been uneventful, and we all left the airport once again with our bags in tow for the 45-minute ride to the hotel. As we drove from the airport to the hotel, the cab driver pointed and showed us the various Olympic venues that we were passing. The cab driver, speaking in broken English, was very excited about the upcoming Olympics and the business it had already brought him. He said all of this with a smile, showing his slightly yellow teeth, with one hand always waving around in the air as if his words alone could not express his excitement enough.

The Grand Hyatt was in the center of Seoul and was set amid eighteen acres of waterfalls and landscaped gardens at the foot of Mt. Namsan. When I walked into the lavish hotel lobby I was embarrassed that I had jeans and a tee shirt on with a loose-fitting jacket. This hotel was exquisite and I felt painfully plain and underdressed. I was equally embarrassed when I entered my room; as the bellman placed my bag in the center of the room, the beauty and tranquility of this room embraced and welcomed me. There were large windows, with stellar views overlooking the city and the hotel gardens below. I tipped the bellman in US currency since I had not had time to exchange money yet.

After our mandatory debriefing meeting, we knew we had the remainder of the day and most of tomorrow free. "George, what was going on at the airport with the police talking to you and then staring at me?" I asked.

"They couldn't believe that you were on our team; being a woman, blonde, beautiful, skinny, and so tall!" he said with a grin.

"Oh, well — guess we had them guessing, didn't we?" I said.

"Yep, you had them going, Maggie," George said.

It was 1400 hours and we were free until 1630 hours the next day. A few of our team members had been to Seoul before and excitedly told me that this was the place to shop. Big Earl said his wife Edith loved the shopping deals you could get here. It was later in the afternoon, but a few of us decided to go to the Itaewon shopping district anyway.

The cultural shock was almost overwhelming. Once we stepped out of the cab we were recognized as tourists and immediately beckoned by the many vendors toward their small shops or carts. And then the bartering began. For hours and hours we walked, shopped, talked, looked, shopped and shopped. So many brand-name clothes, knock-off purses that looked real, eel skin shoes, and custom-made suits, you name it. Everything in apparel was here. Overall, we didn't buy as much as we wanted because we knew we'd be back in Seoul multiple times over the next three weeks, so it was best to shop on our last visit here so we wouldn't have to carry everything from country to country.

We ate dinner at a local restaurant before heading back to the hotel. It was a very interesting day so far from home. I purchased a few postcards in the hotel gift shop, and knowing I could stay up late, when I went up to my room I ordered tea from room service. Once the tea arrived I sat quietly by the window enjoying the view of the flickering city lights and the darkened gardens below while writing postcards to my family. Whenever I traveled, I always tried to send postcards. I loved opening my mailbox and finding more than just bills, so I hoped my family would love getting postcards from me as I began my travels around the world.

The next day I walked through the eighteen-acre garden, watching children play, elderly people walk, and groups participating in tai chi surrounded by waterfalls and beautifully landscaped gardens. I could walk have walked for hours in this beautiful garden, getting the exercise I needed without going out on the busy streets of Hannam 2-Dong yongsan-GU. And out of respect, I didn't want to run in these gardens, because I didn't want to disturb the tranquility of this lush place.

Later that afternoon, we met in the lobby at 1630 hours and repeated the departure process that was going to become rote and very familiar over the weeks ahead. Miles and miles of air time were slipping behind us, with still more miles and miles ahead. In some ways these missions were boring — boring in that we flew uneventful trips repeatedly, yet we always had in the back of our minds that we needed to stay vigilant, silently protecting those citizens of the world that flew aboard these aircraft.

Two weeks had passed and we had flown to and from Seoul, Narita, Singapore, Hong Kong, and Manila at least once. Tonight we were departing from Narita for the fifth or sixth time, heading to Bangkok, Thailand on a flight that left at 2200 hours. The flight was fondly referred to as a "red eye" because we would land early the following morning after a five hour and forty-five-minute flight. No sleeping, just lots of hot coffee!

I was seated in business class, just a few rows behind first class, so I was able to see the cockpit door easily from my location as well as the forward galley and lavatory. This flight was about three quarters full and again I was fortunate not to have anyone sitting next to me. At least I could stretch my legs and arms without knocking the passenger next to me, which was a welcome relief after so much flying. There would be minimal food service on this flight since it was anticipated that most of the passengers would be asleep.

The crew briefings were complete; we taxied, took off, and leveled out for our long flight to Bangkok. I had purchased another book before leaving the Radisson Hotel in Narita. I began making a habit of leaving the books I had finished in the seat back pocket of various flights for other passengers or crewmembers to find and enjoy. There was no sense in traveling around with books that I had read when someone else could enjoy them.

About three hours into the flight, I saw a male passenger moving from the back part of the aircraft toward the front. He passed me in a hurry and every hair on the back of my neck stood up. I immediately got out of my seat and followed him into the first class section, where I saw him open the lavatory door, and disappear inside, with a click as the door was locked. Big Earl, sensing something was different as well, was up on his feet and had moved to the galley adjacent to the lavatory. As he stood in the galley, the first class cabin was to his left and the aircraft cockpit door to his right.

When the passenger came out of the lavatory he turned and started pulling on the cockpit door handle. Big Earl placed his hands on the passenger's shoulders, spun him around, and moved him into the galley with swift precision, which I had never seen from such a big guy. Earl was in charge, patting the man down before either one of them spoke. I moved forward and stood between the passenger and the cockpit door. Big Earl began to question him about what he was doing. Once Big Earl and I were in close proximity we noticed that the man reeked of alcohol as he began babbling in very broken English. Big Earl knew some Japanese, Korean, and Thai, because he had spent several years in Asia when he was in the military and had a gift for languages. So the two of them were able to communicate enough to figure out that the man had a great deal to drink, both while waiting for the flight prior to boarding at the airport in Narita, and then again onboard. He desperately needed to use the restroom and since the back lavatories were occupied he decided to use the front one. Now we understood why the man was in such a hurry. Then after relieving himself, he thought he might get a tour of the cockpit.

Big Earl looked over the man's shoulder at me, and I said, "Let's hold him here for a few minutes while I check out the lavatory." I turned, and before entering the lavatory, a third agent moved forward to replace me as Big Earl's back-up. I thoroughly trashed the lavatory in search of any possible explosive devices, finding none.

By now the passenger was a pale shade of white and looked pretty shaken up and worried that he was in serious trouble. The third agent and I escorted the man back to his seat, as inconspicuously as possible, searched his seat area, took down his carry-on luggage, and moved to the back of the aircraft to search it. Everything turned up negative and we were pretty convinced that that man was indeed drunk and had no malicious intent. Big Earl stayed with him for the remainder of the flight, and I returned to my seat.

Over the next hour we briefed George, our team leader, the captain, and the chief flight attendant of the events that had occurred on the flight. Upon arrival in Bangkok the airport police arrived and escorted the now-sober passenger off the aircraft. After several more hours of report writing, and multiple calls back to Washington, DC, the team was able to leave the airport and head for the hotel. Our destination was the Millennium Hilton Hotel that towered majestically above the Chao Praya River. The 45-minute traffic-fiiled gridlock between the airport and the hotel would have made driving in Los Angeles feel like driving on back country roads. Cars, motorcycles, buses, and bicycles all ignored every traffic light, stop sign, and police command in their bid to be first. It was madness. The traffic and pollution were astounding. I immediately knew there would be no running outside for me in this city of hustle and bustle.

Fortunately for George, Big Earl, and I, we had thirty-six hours on the ground before we headed back to Narita. This was the last leg before the long flight back to Seattle. After our arrival at the hotel, more telephone calls, and paperwork being moved back and forth between Washington, DC and the nearby US Embassy, we were close to being done for the day. Finally, by early afternoon we headed back to the hotel. If we could, we wanted to go shopping!

Where Seoul was the shopping Mecca for apparel and goods, Bangkok was the Mecca for semi-precious stones and gold. I loved jewelry, especially rings, so I was all for shopping before we left this hectic, people-packed city. The front desk recommended a shopping center very close to the hotel that was open until midnight. The bell captain on duty summoned a taxi for us. George didn't want to go shopping, but Big Earl and I did, so off we went on our late-afternoon adventure.

I found when I was in the company of Big Earl, no one bothered me. The man was a giant among men, and I felt very much protected and totally at ease shopping with him. I was happy to have the company. I purchased several loose stones, a sapphire and diamond channel cut ring in 18 carat gold, and an emerald cut topaz ring for my mom. I had never owed such beautiful pieces of jewelry, so I was ecstatic with my purchases. Big Earl found some topaz earrings for his wife and he was very pleased with the quality and the prices. All of the store owners gave us their business cards in hopes that we would return or refer other Americans to their shops.

It was close to midnight when we arrived back at the hotel and we were leaving the next day at 11:30 a.m.

The next day, our flight to Narita was calm and quiet, unlike the last trip, and everyone breathed a sigh of relief when we deplaned later that evening. This would be our last night in Narita, as we would be heading back to Seattle tomorrow, and Big Earl and I were catching a late flight back to Los Angeles. Big Earl's wife, Edith, was meeting him at the airport, so he offered to give me a ride home, which I gladly accepted.

We all decided to go back to a small local restaurant, a short walk to from the hotel, and have a meal together. I loved this little place, called the Gioizza Bar, where you sat on the floor on mats and tucked your feet beneath you. Chop sticks, big bowls or rice, soup and gioizza (pot stickers in English) to your heart's content. I didn't drink beer, so I passed on the Kirin and had a Coke with my meal. Even that was a treat for me, since I rarely drank sodas at home.

Stuffed to the gills, we all waddled back to the hotel, enjoying the cool night air and chatting away about this trip, which for some of us was our first mission. This would be our last opportunity to chat as a group, because once we arrived in the hotel lobby in the morning it was all business from there on, and we knew when we arrived in Seattle we'd all be preoccupied with getting back home. This flock was about to separate like SandHill Cranes do when they lose their mate and never mate again. It was a joyful time that we had together these past three weeks, but also a melancholy time, for we knew this mission was coming to an end.

The ten and a half hour flight back to Seattle seemed like an eternity. Big Earl and I were in business class, so we were much more comfortable than some of the team, but we were still antsy to get home and see our family and friends.

The difference between this trip and any other that we had flown during the last three weeks was that after landing we all stayed on the aircraft and let all of the other passengers deplane. Once the flight was clear, the cabin crew held off the cleaners for a few minutes while the team debriefed, and unloaded and secured our weapons. Once again, we were no longer in federal air marshal status and needed to surrender our firearms to their safe positions and be prepared to stow them in our hard-sided checked baggage.

We deplaned, found our luggage, cleared customs, and proceeded to find someplace to discreetly move our firearms into our checked luggage before we dashed off to various airline ticket counters to check in for our flights home.

Once Big Earl and I arrived in Los Angeles, we officially went off the time clock one hour after landing. Edith met her husband as planned just outside the Alaska Airlines terminal, lower level, with the car in idle, as big kisses and hugs were exchanged between the two of them. I was envious, since I didn't have anyone to meet me with a big hug and a warm kiss. Big Earl introduced me to his wife as we stuffed our luggage into the back of their SUV, and we exited the airport chattering away about our experiences and realizing how tired we were.

Unlocking my door, I stumbled into my cozy beach cottage, happy to be home. Once again I changed and went for a short run, because I knew if I didn't do it now I wouldn't run today. It was still early enough that I needed to try and stay up and sleep later so I could get used to the time change again and get back on track, as it was Friday afternoon and I had to go back to work on Monday.

I decided to run a few miles down along the beach and then backtrack into the Rivera to shop at Trader Joe's for a few essentials, and then pick up my mail before the post office closed for the day. It was a picture-perfect day and exactly what I needed. I was elated to be home and I felt a real sense of accomplishment.

Once I got home, I quickly sorted through my mail to see what was urgent and what wasn't. I unpacked, and cooked dinner while having a glass of Two Buck Chuck red wine, as it was fondly called. It was fairly decent wine made by Charles Shaw and cost a $1.98, hence the name Two Buck Chuck.

I was home; I was exhausted, happy, and buzzed from not having any wine for three weeks. It was time for Maggie Stewart to get some sleep. I knew I was going to be home only for a week before I was scheduled to go to training in Oklahoma City, so it was imperative that I get back on schedule sooner rather than later.

When I arrived at the office on Monday, I was greeted by Agent Stanton, Big Earl, and the rest of the staff as if I were a long-lost buddy. It was wonderful to be back; I chatted with Stanton and the rest of the team for about fifteen minutes before the manager, Cindy, arrived for work and sent everyone scurrying back to their desks just at the sight of her. She said good morning and we all said good morning before we drifted off to our desks. Jet lag had been nipping at my toes and body since my return from my mission, so I kept the coffee flowing through most of the morning.

The week passed at rapid speed once again. The post-trip paperwork wasn't too bad, since most of it had been accomplished during the trip. George, our team leader, was a wizard at completing time cards; throughout the trip, as part of our daily debrief, we also got in the habit of completing them. I understood the importance once I got back to the field office. The data entry that Kelly had to perform after all of these trips was complicated, so having the time cards done as the work hours were performed made everyone's time card accurate and exact. This was sage advice that I would remember for future trips.

I said goodbye once again to Agent Stanton on my way out the door on Friday afternoon, for I was off to another adventure coming that Monday. I was leaving on Sunday for my four-week training in Oklahoma City to officially earn my credentials to become a special agent. After that graduation I would officially be able to independently conduct airline, airport, and screening inspections, and audits and tests on my own. Agent Stanton and I would still be partnered together, but I would be more of an asset now because I would be fully trained. Again, I was really excited to complete this phase of my training and probation as a new employee.

Oklahoma City Yacht Club

I WAS PACKED, ready, and waiting outside for the taxi that I had called to take me to the airport. After being gone for three weeks, I suddenly realized a few days ago that it was going to be even harder to pack for a trip lasting four weeks. I tried to make a list of everything I needed, eventually giving up because I kept losing the list. Besides, I figured out during one sleepless night that if I did forget anything, it would be easy enough to find a Target or a K-Mart for emergency shopping since I was going to Oklahoma, not Asia. "It will be just fine, Maggie Stewart, just fine," I mumbled, half awake and half asleep.

The taxi was on time, and I arrived at LAX's Terminal 4, American Airlines, an hour and a half before my scheduled departure. I paid the cabby, asking for a receipt in order to accurately voucher my travel expenses, and got in line at the curbside podium so I could check my bag in and get my boarding pass. The check-in process was quickly accomplished and I was through the checkpoint screening and on my way to my departure gate in about thirty minutes. Finally I could relax, get a cup of coffee, buy a magazine and people-watch before boarding the MD-80 that would carry me from LAX to DFW, where I would have to switch flights and take a regional jet from DFW to OKC.

Coffee in hand and my *Runner's World* magazine tucked into my carry-on bag, I stood, rather than sat, to watch the airline world around me. I had always loved aviation, ever since I was a little girl. I wanted to get on any airplane, fly to any destination, logging mile after mile, while chatting, meeting new people, and learning about the world around me. It was always the draw of the excitement, the mystery, and the magic that I knew had to be mingled among the many airlines seats and all those passengers seated in them that made me love flying so much.

While I was in the Navy, I was assigned flight attendant duties as a part-time crew member on a turbo propeller Convair 340 air-craft (CV-340) that the base commander used on a regular basis. On that medium-sized 51-seat passenger aircraft, I flew throughout the Caribbean over the course of a year, going from island to island. For many flights we'd be on the ground for just a few hours, during which I was responsible for refueling the aircraft, so I usually never left the airport. I did weight and balances, pre-flight and post-flight prepara-tions, along with cooking some terrible meals while waiting for the base commander to return. When in flight, I chatted with the pas-sengers on board, who were mostly military personnel traveling back and forth between islands for various reasons. The aircraft was old, the interior ugly and dilapidated, but it was a free ride to Jamaica, Gautama Bay, Haiti, Santo Domingo, and many other islands that were full of charm, beauty, rum, and sometimes poverty.

When I got out of the Navy I was hired by an airline in St. Croix that was flying CV-440s between the islands of St. Thomas and St. Croix. The CV-440 was a newer model than the CV-330, but it still leaked oil like a sieve. It was a lucky break for me, both deciding to join the military, and then getting the opportunity to fly as a crew member. *I've had lots of luck and great opportunities since my mili-tary service that's for sure*, I thought, and my life was spectacular.

Once our flight landed, and as we taxied toward the gate, I looked at my itinerary to find the flight number for my connecting flight. I ex-ited the jetway, looked at the monitors in the terminal for my flight, and began walking toward the departure gate. I had almost an hour between connections and about twenty gates to walk in the terminal, but I had plenty of time to get to the next gate. I only had a small backpack with me, and as I walked, I hoped my gigantic check-in bag was following my footsteps in the baggage maze below the main terminals. As I approached the gate, I could see Big Earl standing in the gate area, along with Georgia and Colleen.

"Hey, hello," I said, and everyone's voices rose to a loud pitch as we hugged and greeted one another, and a number of people looked around to see what the ruckus was all about. The regional jet that was flying us from DFW to OKC carried only nineteen passengers, so our joy was viewed as disruptive in the tiny lounge area.

Colleen was based at the New York Office, Georgia at the Washington, DC Dulles Office, and Earl and I were in the Los Angeles Office, so we all had a lot of catching up to do over the next month. The flight was called and we all boarded the thirty-minute flight to OKC.

Colleen and I sat next to each other, and even though we hadn't spoken since leaving FAM training, we felt like we were long-lost friends catching up on life. After FAM training, and back in New York, Colleen had gotten engaged to her long-time boyfriend, who still worked for the FBI. He had surprised her during a run in New York's Central Park by pretending he had a sore knee on the return leg of their run, and convinced her that they needed to take a horse-drawn carriage ride back to where their car was parked. Once he got her into the carriage, he got down on the sore knee and asked her to marry him. It was a fairy-tale story and I was so happy for Colleen. She was beaming the entire time we talked.

It felt like we had just barely taken off before we were landing again. The flight was bumpy as we headed north across the open plains between Texas and Oklahoma in the small regional jet that found every air pocket possible along its flight route. So we were all very happy to deplane down the small steps and walk across the ramp and into the terminal.

We all collected our luggage and waited for the hotel shuttle to take us to the hotel. The conversations continued, and it seemed we would never run out of stories about how we were all doing and how much we already loved our jobs. For many of us, this was a dream job, full of travel, challenges, and many, many opportunities.

The following morning we all met in the Residence Inn hotel lobby. Earl and Colleen had rented cars, so we all carpooled to the training facility together, which was about ten miles from the hotel. The drive was easy compared to New York, Washington, or Los Angeles.

Once we arrived at the Federal Aviation Administration's Mike Monroney Aeronautical Training Center, a security guard checked all of our government IDs, then cleared us all onto the facility and gave us a parking pass for the day. Both Earl and Colleen would need to go to the main security office and get a parking pass for the month, the guard told us. He gave us a map of the facility and indicated where our classrooms were located. None of us knew where we were going, but we eventually found our way, like lost sheep heading home, and arrived on time for class.

"Here we go again," I said to Colleen as we took seats toward the back of the class. She smiled, nodding her head, and our day began.

Agent Stanton had taught me well, as I discovered early in the first week of training. We conducted classroom tabletop exercises where we discussed various security scenarios and the teams we were divided into were graded on their knowledge of airport and security programs and ability to resolve various security breaches, along with ability to demonstrate communication skills at every level found in an airport environment, from top CEOs to other government agencies.

Every Friday we were tested on the skills and written materials we had studied during the week. All of these exams were pass or fail. If you failed, you had one opportunity to retake the exam. If you failed a second time, you were washed out of the program and sent home. If you were a government employee still on probation, you would be released from government service like a fish at a catch-and-release pond. Everyone in our training class of twenty-six agents all had less than a year on the job and we were all on probation, so we quickly learned to form study groups that met during the week and on Sunday afternoons.

Saturdays became our day to do laundry and sightsee around Oklahoma City. I discovered that Oklahoma was more than a big flat state situated in the middle of the US. There was a lot to do and see here. Oklahoma City is the capital and the largest city in the state of Oklahoma. Livestock, oil, and government employees make up a large segment of the local economy. The city is situated in the middle of an active oil field, and oil derricks dot the capitol grounds. "Bricktown" is the entertainment district, with water taxis that will take you to restaurants and other various activities along the canal.

During the second week of our training, John, an agent from Kansas City, and I were talking during lunch about what everyone was doing this weekend. John said he was an avid sailor and wanted to rent a Lido 14 from the nearby yacht harbor at Lake Hefner. I knew how to sail too, so we decided to rent a boat on Saturday afternoon for a few hours. We raised our hands in a high-five, smiling in agreement that sailing in Oklahoma would indeed be different. The beach girl said out loud, "Who sails in Oklahoma?" Guess we were about to find out.

John and I agreed to meet the next morning in the hotel lobby at 9:00 a.m. I made a mental note to check the weather report when we got out of class, and then decide what gear I would bring. We were already well into September, but the average high every day here had been in the 90s so far, with lows in the 60s. As long as there wasn't any rain in the forecast, it would be perfect sailing weather. It had been years since I last sailed, but I was looking forward to getting back out on the water.

John was waiting in the lobby, as agreed, when I walked through the lobby door Saturday morning at 9:00 a.m. He was wearing navy-blue shorts, a white shirt that was in need of a bleaching, and a floppy tan hat. You could tell by his big grin that he was really looking forward to a day of sailing. I, on the other hand, wore a pair of nylon running shorts, a white tee shirt, and a pair of tennis shoes. I had a small backpack with me filled with a hat, sunscreen, a small towel, a couple of sandwiches, and fruit.

The short drive to Lake Hefner passed quickly, for there were very few cars out early on a Saturday morning. The parking lot at the recreational facility was about half full and you could already see a few small sailboats rocking amidst the small waves that continually moved in an easterly direction across the lake. Our car doors slammed shut simultaneously and we began walking over in search of a sailboat to rent.

We approached a small dock with a booth that looked like a place to buy tickets to the local carnival show. It was painted in several different colors, and had every patch of paint looking like it was in desperate need of a touch-up, except for the large sign that hung above the glass sales window that said boats, paddle boats, and kayaks for rent. The young man in the sales office looked to be in his mid-twenties; he had sandy blond hair and a sunburnt nose, with a few freckles scattered across his face. He looked happy behind his glass wall, with his cell phone, and a soda can propped in front of him. He was texting when we walked up to the window, but politely stopped when he realized we were potential customers.

John inquired about the kind of small "day" sailboats that were available for rent and what the prices were. The young man told us that most of the boats had already been rented due to a Cub Scout outing and merit badge event that was going on, and that most of the small boats were already rented for the day. He told us that the only boat he had left was a Lido 14. I let John know that was perfect for me, since I had learned to sail on a Lido as a kid. I admitted it had been awhile since I had sailed, but I was very confident that I would regain my skills quickly.

In exchange for $100 in cash and our driver's license to ensure our returning the boat, we were quickly led down the dock to where the Lido sat quietly in the early morning. The young man showed us where the life vests were, gave us a general explanation of the equipment onboard, and began to depart. I stopped him before he left and said I couldn't resist asking why the sales booth he was working in was painted so many colors.

He laughed and said, "Well, the local college kids painted the booth these colors a few months ago during spring break, as a prank, and no one has bothered to repaint it since." He continued, "I think the owner of the yacht club actually likes the paint job, but won't admit it to anyone."

We saw another customer walking up to his booth, so he waved us off as he bounded up the dock toward the people that were waiting.

John stepped into the boat first, and I followed suit. I immediately noticed that this boat was almost as dilapidated as the orange carpet in my office in LA. The small white deck and white hull with blue waterline stripes were dull and faded. As I looked around her, I could see she needed to be cleaned up and the wood varnished. The mast, boom, and fittings looked worn as well. But the main sail that was rolled up on the mast waiting to be set free looked brand-new, along with the jib. I put my cooler down, pulled my hat tighter down on my head, and decided to see if this little lady could race.

The Lido 14 dinghy was built to be a family day-sailer that can seat as many as six but is really more comfortable with two or three people. This boat was never designed to be a race boat, but owners of these slim little boats got together and raced one another regularly; sailing clubs and race events were soon formed throughout the United States and parts of Mexico. They really are fun when they get going.

We pushed away from the dock while raising the main sail. We sailed straight out to begin catching the wind that was starting to blow off the lake. John was sailing, and so far he seemed to know what he was doing. I told him I was going forward slightly to raise the jib, so we'd have two sails for more speed.

As we moved across the choppy waters, the wooden centerboard moved, slightly vibrating as if to officially record its protest at pulling through the water against the flow of nature. John held the tiller in his left hand as he leaned up back against the starboard side of the boat. John eventually shouted, "Coming about," and I ducked under the boom as the little Lido turned gracefully and headed off once again.

This little boat was pretty bare-bones, with only two life preservers onboard, two tattered seat cushions, and the sail bag stowed in the front of the boat. John and I took turns sailing back and forth across Lake Hefner over the next few hours. The wind was in our favor the first three hours of our sail, but as we turned to head back to the yacht club, she had a change of heart. The wind on the lake came to a complete standstill as the doldrums left us lifeless in the middle of a lake, like a puddle of melted ice cream on a summer sidewalk.

John looked at me and I could see the look of confidence he had espoused all day begin to fade as quickly as the wind had just done. I immediately said, "It will be okay," and started recommending different visual land points to sail toward as we very, very, slowly crawled across the lake. When we got close to land I could see that we were still quite a distance from the spot we were supposed to dock at. I told John we need to come about again so we could tack back and forth and inch our way farther north and up along the lake's coast. I estimated we were about a half-mile from our dock.

John came about immediately and as we caught just a taste of wind, he asked, "Hey, Maggie, is this supposed to happen?" as he held the tiller up in his hand. With the tiller broken, we drifted aimlessly, running aground on a sandbar; then the centerboard stuck in the sticky lake mud. The boat came to an immediate stop. Now John was really beginning to get upset. I told him we had to get out of the boat and push it off the sandbar, re-board, and we'd be fine. But John refused to get out of the boat, saying he was terrified of the water! "Really?" I said as I looked at him in complete disbelief and a bit of distain. He only nodded his head in affirmation and I knew, at that moment, that John was not going to get out of the boat.

So over the side I went, feet first, into the murky and cold lake water. "Icky," I screeched. My blouse filled with air, like a makeshift life vest, before it and I were completely wet. I walked on the soft, squishy lake mud to the bow, and grabbed the line tied to the bow of the boat. I never liked swimming in lakes; the dark, murky, muddy water always gave me the creeps, and now I was walking on the bottom of this lake. Needless to say, I was not completely pleased with this turn of events. With one hand on the line, and one hand on the port side of the boat, I began to push the Lido, all 310 pounds of her hull weight, along with John's 240 pounds. I soon realized I was probably going to lose this battle! But I was determined to try, and I began yelling to John at the top of my lungs, shouting: "Pull up the centerboard!"

He finally figured out what I was yelling about, and I could hear him pulling and tugging on the centerboard. I continued to push the boat in a forward direction with all of my strength and might, and after a few tough physically spent minutes I could feel the boat lifting ever so slightly as she began to lift and move away from the sandbar. She finally freed herself, but I continued to walk with the boat until she was deep enough in the water that I was beginning to swim breast stroke style. It was time for me to get back into the boat.

Ahead of me I could see several Ring-billed Gulls bobbing up and down watching us and our boat with their yellow eyes with red rims. I suspected they were trying to decide if we had any potential food. These birds are opportunistic scavengers and will forage anywhere to get insects, fish, grain, eggs, earthworms, and even rodents. I probably looked like a large rodent at this point, so I eyed them in return. These gulls are migratory and should have been moving toward the Gulf of Mexico by now, but maybe the food around here was just too tempting to migrate. They continued to float lazily in the water as I began swimming along the port side of the boat.

I hollered at John, "Point the boat into the wind so she won't sail away without me."

As I came up alongside the boat, John reached down and grabbed my left forearm and began lifting me out of the water as I kicked my feet and pulled my body up with my right arm. As quickly as I was out of the boat I was back in, but this time I was freezing and furious. John looked at me with a sheepish look and I grabbed the small towel I had brought with me and dried off as best I could. As soon as I dried off, I took over command and limped the Lido safely back to our dock.

When we had her safely tied up, the young man who had rented us the boat this morning met us at the dock and made sure the Lido was tied up properly and that the life vests, sail bag, and two seat cushions were still in the boat.

"Look," I said to the young man. I showed him the broken tiller and let him know that perhaps they should look into a little better maintenance program for these lovely boats, or perhaps find them a better home. Lido 14s held a special place in my heart since I had learned sail on them many years ago.

"Okay," he said. "I'll tell the boss."

We collected our driver's licenses and headed for the car. By then I was dry but looking a little worse for wear, with a thin layer of mud covering my legs, dripping dry dirt clots from my clothes, and I was getting hungry — really, really hungry.

John sensed that I was hungry, or perhaps he was just trying to make up for me getting into the muddy lake and bailing our butts out of a jam, so he offered to buy me dinner. Oklahoma City is an oil town and a cow town, so in my mind I pictured a nice steak dinner, with a big baked potato with the works and a green salad. I looked at John and said, "Okay, I think that's the least you can do for me after this sailing adventure."

"Great," he said as he pulled away from the yacht club. A few minutes later we turned onto Meridian Avenue, the main street through this part of town, and the street our hotel was on. Before we got to the hotel John pulled into the Waffle House parking lot and parked right in front. *So much for a steak dinner*, I said to myself.

Come Monday morning the story of the weekend sailing adventure was told multiple times, and everyone joined in the fun of giving John a hard time for staying in the boat and then taking me to the Waffle House for dinner. John was a real trooper and took everything in stride. And I knew this was an adventure that I would never forget. Sailing in Oklahoma turned out to be pretty unique after all.

The next two weeks were spent studying in groups, independently, and conducting airport incident tabletop exercises and testing. It was a grueling two weeks with lots of coffee flowing morning, noon, and night. Again, we knew the importance of our jobs, our duty to protect the traveling public, and our mission. This training was essential to our abilities to properly conduct airport and airline inspections, both domestically and internationally. The pace was unforgiving, but the mission demanded it.

As we were finishing up class, only two days away from graduation, our class coordinator rushed into our classroom and abruptly interrupted us by directing our instructor to turn on the television to the local news station.

Tragedy struck again today on December 21st, 1988 with the bombing of Pan Am 103 over Lockerbie, Scotland. The B-747 flying from London's Heathrow Airport bound for John F. Kennedy Airport in New York had 243 passengers onboard and 16 crew members when it exploded at 31,000 feet.

The air traffic controller working the flight saw one radar echo turn into five as the plane erupted into a fireball and radar contact was lost. Those five radar echoes again reminded us of the importance of our jobs and why we had become a cadre of air marshals protecting US airlines around the world.

We still had a final exam to take, which would be scored after lunch, and we would be notified if we passed or not. We all were preoccupied with the recent crash, but we also knew we needed to graduate in order to prevent further tragedies like yesterday's attack against aviation. We had studied hard all month, so we all felt confident in our knowledge and felt prepared. I was tapping my pencil rapidly on my desk in anxious anticipation. "I'm ready," I said to myself. "Maggie Stewart, you're ready."

The following morning was our last day in Oklahoma City, and once the Director of Civil Aviation Security (ACS), Director Sword, had flown in from Washington, DC, it was to preside over a much more somber graduation ceremony this time. There were not any top honors in this training program; it was pass or fail. The twenty-four agents that began training four weeks earlier had all successfully completed their training. Each one of us individually was presented with our Special Agent Credentials, along with a hearty handshake from the director and the instructors. However, the urgency of our returning home, although unspoken, remained in the forefront of all of our minds. Each of us knew that our work had taken on another level of importance, and we were all anxious to get to the airport and head back to our home offices.

I knew that very busy times were ahead for all of us.

I now knew beyond a shadow of a doubt that all of the agents standing in this classroom were about to become very busy with the implementation of many new aviation security changes, both domestically and internationally, after these two aviation attacks barely a year apart: the first a domestic "insider threat" attack with the downing of PSA 1771, by a disgruntled employee; and now Pam Am 103, an act of terrorism.

The holiday season, like last year, was tainted with sadness and an urgency to ensure the FAA's new regulations and security measures were implemented immediately.

We all quickly and quietly said our farewells and headed for the airport, knowing that these tragedies would change the course of our careers forever.

Learning the Ropes

I ARRIVED AT LAX Airport and took the luxury of grabbing a taxi for the ten-mile ride from the airport to my apartment. The cabbie was totally dissatisfied with the short fare, but there wasn't much he could say about it, or not say about it, except to give me the silent treatment. At LAX, taxis go into a queue, and the fare that comes up for them is completely out of their control, so there was no point in taking it out on me. I think that thought occurred to him a few miles before we arrived at my place, when he realized his bad attitude might be impacting his tip. He began speaking to me about the beautiful weather and the beaches in the area. I agreed with his assessment as we arrived at the address I had provided him.

When taking taxis, I have always been in the habit of giving them an address that is about a block away from my actual home address. As a single person, I always thought it was better to not be too specific about my destination; besides, I never minded walking. I paid my bill, asked for a receipt, and gave the driver a moderate tip before he sped away. I assumed he was trying to get back into the queue at the airport as quickly as he could.

My flight had departed from Oklahoma City at 3:00 p.m. with a one-hour stop in Dallas/Fort Worth so I could change aircraft for my final leg to Los Angeles. I had landed at LAX at 5:00 p.m., making up two hours with the time change from Central Standard Time to Pacific

Standard Time. It was already dark, but The Strand along the beach had street lights, so I knew I could run anytime. I needed to run, for I was antsy, ready to report for work, but I had two days to wait it out until Monday, so a run was just what I needed right about now.

It's time to get the wiggles out, Maggie; it's beyond time to go for a run, I thought.

I quickly dropped my bag inside my apartment door, changed into my running gear, and off I went, heading toward the beach. Winter had firmly arrived and I was thankful that I wore long pants, a long-sleeved shirt and a jacket, for the wind off the ocean was bitterly cold.

I looked down at the beach and saw hundreds of seagulls sitting on the beach with their heads and necks slightly tucked in and their feathers fluffed up so they could stay warm. Maybe I should have stayed in, but I had been sitting either in an airport or airplane all day, so I was ready to breathe in some fresh air. I ran along The Strand, heading north toward the Redondo Beach Pier. I did my usual three-mile run at a much quicker pace than my normal twelve-minute mile pace, actually almost breaking ten-minute miles as I zoomed past homes and apartment buildings that were built to enjoy the ocean view. I was spent by the time I got home, but ran quickly when I heard my home telephone ringing.

"Hello, this is Maggie," I said.

"Are you ready to get to work?" Special Agent Stanton boomed out from the telephone receiver.

"More than ready," I said.

"Good. Be at the office at 0600 sharp tomorrow morning, and I'll show you what's been happening in the past couple of days. Unlimited overtime has been authorized; new security measures are coming out from our policy and operational staffers in DC, and you need to be at work sooner rather than later." He said all of this with one breath.

"I'll be there," I said.

"Good. See you in the morning." And the line went silent.

"Now that's what I'm talking about," I said as I danced around the room, knowing now that I could immediately go to work. With that notion in mind, I quickly began unpacking my bag, plopping everything into piles of white or dark colors so I could start doing my laundry. The one luxury, a necessity for me, was having a washer and dryer in my apartment. I was very fortunate to find an apartment complex that included a stack-up washer and dryer in the kitchen for an additional $35 per month. The rent was more expensive, but it was worth washing my clothes in a machine that only I was going to use, and I didn't have to carry baskets full of laundry back and forth from the apartment.

As the whites began agitating around and around in the washing machine, like I was agitating around in my apartment, I went online to send a note to the post office so my mail service could resume on Monday. I also requested that all of the mail that had been placed on hold be delivered as well. This was a free service from the post office and I was very happy to take advantage of it, as it saved me from going down to the post office on Redondo Street to pick up my mail. "Another luxury, you spoiled girl," I said, smiling to myself.

"Now, what to eat for dinner?" was my next question to myself. I had stopped and quickly picked up a few things at the store before I came back to the apartment from my run. Not much; stuff to make a salad with, and of course my normal coffee items. I have recently discovered Starbucks Breakfast Blend coffee, and it had quickly become a favorite of mine. I poured myself a glass of white wine and began making a salad. I had some bread in the freezer, so I thawed a couple of pieces in the microwave and then popped them into the toaster to brown.

I sat down to watch some TV, enjoy the comforts of home and a home-cooked meal, though it was only a salad. I moved the laundry from the washer to the dryer, put in another load, and finished up the dishes all before calling it a day.

I was still jumpy, but having a meal in me and a glass of wine running through me, I could feel my pulse slowing down and my thoughts beginning to slow from a sprinter's pace to a marathon pace as I got ready for bed.

The drive in the morning would be quick and easy without any weekday traffic to worry about, so I set my alarm clock for 0500 hours, knowing that I would easily be able to get up, dress, and be out the door in thirty minutes. My apartment was a fifteen-minute drive from the field office, so I would have plenty of time.

When I arrived at the office at 0550, the parking lot was full and I could see several of the other agents from the office already walking toward the building that had not yet seen the sunrise.

Agent Stanton was there, and when he saw me, he walked over to me and gave me a pat on the back and welcomed me back. Everyone in the office was milling around the center of the "pit," waiting for Supervisor Drake to arrive. Agent Stanton began filling me in on what had happened since last Thursday's tragedy aboard Pam AM 103, coupled with the additional security measures we would be implementing here in the US.

Agent Stanton explained out loud, saying, "Late Friday, as you were flying home, Director Sword sent out a message through his office, the Director of Operations, in Washington, DC, that immediate and swift action was going to occur over the next several weeks in policy changes and security procedures for both the airlines and the airports, along with additional security measures and techniques being implemented at every checkpoint in the United States."

Agent Stanton further explained that Director Sword understood that staffing was critically short and that unlimited overtime had been authorized, and he was in direct contact with the Office of Personnel Management and the Human Resource Department within the FAA and ACS to hire additional special agents and support services staff, because now we had security threats both domestically and internationally.

Agent Stanton said, "When Supervisor Drake arrives, he's going to tell us what changes have occurred now that new security directives have been issued. This should be interesting."

The airlines were currently responsible for checkpoint screening, in that they directly contracted security companies to conduct screening for them. The hiring, classroom, and on-the-job training were all managed by the various security screening companies, but the airlines were responsible to the FAA for compliance with the FAA regulations pertaining to screening. All of the changes that came from the FAA were directed at the airlines, but they in return had to ensure that the screening companies complied.

The airport had their own set of federal security requirements regarding fencing security, ramp and terminal security, employee badges, and various other areas that needed to be protected.

"After the crash of PSA 1771 last year, the FAA had mandated several security changes for both the airlines and the airports that you didn't notice since you were still a newbie. Now that a domestic threat and an international threat have occurred in just a little over a year, the FAA is working beyond overtime to get security measures written and in place to protect our national air space system. It's all going to be expensive for the airlines and airports, but necessary," Agent Stanton said. "Those changes are being disseminated in the form of security directives, which we were waiting to receive from Supervisor Drake. Get ready — hard work, long hours, and overtime galore from this point on."

"Okay," I said. "I'm ready to get to work."

Supervisor Drake arrived in the office around 0630 with stacks of papers in his hand. He said "Good morning" to everyone while putting the stack of papers on the table in the center of the pit. It was our conference room. Drake went and quickly got a cup of coffee and motioned everyone to grab a chair and sit down because this was probably going to take a while, and he looked at the stack of papers and patted them with the palm of his left hand.

He asked Kelly, who also had come in to work, to please roll the portable chalkboard from where it was standing near the kitchen. Agent Stanton got up and helped Kelly move the board to the center of the room.

Supervisor Drake wiped the board clean by rubbing the blue,

pink, and white chalk away with an eraser in quick rapid strokes, indicating he had most likely done this a million times before. It made me wonder what he had done for a living before coming to work for the government.

Drake said, "I'm going to talk first and hand out papers later. Right now I don't want anyone flipping through papers; I just want you all to listen. This is a first for all of us, getting so many security directives at one time, and the work load, as you will soon learn, will be horrendous. So listen up for now, jot down your questions, and if I don't answer them during the briefing we'll cover them at the end.

"As I see it, these security directives have created a two-phase process that we need to follow and implement. Phase one consists of three critical security functions that we need to do; first we're going to test every walk-through metal detector for operational effectiveness, and second we're going to test every x-ray machine for its operational effectiveness. If the equipment we test is fully functional, we are going to place an FAA Certificate Placard on each piece of equipment with the date that it was certified and who certified it. This is a first for our organization and for the government. As you all know, the airlines are responsible for this function, but because of two horrific terrorist incidents; sadly one occurring here in California, and the other in Scotland, FAA Security now wants to establish a baseline for every security machine in the country."

Agent Drake took a sip of his tepid coffee, and continued on by saying, "The testing protocol conducted by special agents all around the country is how we are going to establish this baseline. Third, we're going to record the location and the type of each piece of equipment. This phase has to be completed between now and next Friday. Seems easy? Don't forget, team, that we have sixteen airports spread across the states of Hawaii, Nevada, California, and Arizona. And not every airport has an agent stationed at the airport we need to visit, so be prepared to pack your bags. I'll give you the breakdown of who's going where, later in this briefing.

"Once we collect all of our data, we will forward it to the Regional

Office here in LA and they we'll compile all of the information for our region and forward it to Washington, DC. From what I understand, it is DC's intent to start a national database so they know what equipment is where.

"The second phase strictly involves airport operations, in that we have been asked to oversee each airport in conducting identification badge reconciliation, and for those small airports that have used personal recognition in the past as an identification media process, to see that they establish an employee badge system for their airport. Washington, DC has given us three months to fully implement this security directive. So forget any vacation time (leave) that you may have scheduled, because as of this morning it's being rescinded. Your summer plans might be all right, but I wouldn't plan on having any time off for spring break in April either. We have unlimited overtime now and believe me, I think we're going to need it."

With that he turned to Kelly and asked her to hand out the documents that were sitting on top of the rickety conference table. "Okay, everyone — let's take a ten-minute break so I can get some coffee, and make a few phone calls to ensure nothing has changed in the last hour! Be back in ten, guys," he said as he walked away.

I left the documents that Kelly handed to me on my chair and slipped away to the ladies' room. When I returned, everyone was either sipping a cup of coffee and talking quietly or reading what Kelly had handed to us.

Written on the top and bottom of each document were the words "Sensitive Information" and "For Official Use Only." In the upper right-hand corner was a number in bold print. I immediately found out the reason for the numbering shortly after a sign-in log was handed to me by the agent sitting next to me. These documents were numbered and once the number on the front pages of the sensitive document was matched up with your name, you became one hundred percent responsible for that document. It could not be lost, copied, stolen, or in any way misplaced. No excuses. The documents we had signed for were the changes that were about to be levied upon both the airlines and the airport operators, and it was considered sensitive and could not be shared with anyone except the regulated parties that were being impacted by the changes.

Supervisor Drake returned with another cup of coffee in his hand and advised us that he had spoken to the staff at the regional office, and so far no other updates or changes had been sent from Washington, DC.

"So let's get down to answering any immediate questions. I know there will be more after everyone has had time to read the security directives, but for now let's move on with mapping out a plan for agent deployment. But first, are there any questions?"

All of the agents looked around at one another, and no questions were asked at this time. I think everyone needed some time to digest this new information, and wanted to see the deployment schedule as well.

Drake began pointing to a map that had been taped to the chalkboard. The map was encased in plastic so you could write on it with a marker and not damage it. Drake began drawing circles around various airport clusters and assigning various agents to cover those particular airports. Agent Stanton and I were assigned Los Angeles International Airport, Burbank, Long Beach, Palmdale, and Ontario Airports. So we didn't have to fly anywhere for this assignment, and we would be able to go home at the end of every day as well.

Once we were dismissed from the briefing, Agent Stanton and I began discussing strategies for our deployment to all of these airports. I suggested we go to the outlying airports first since they were farther away but smaller, so the inspection time would be less. Burbank, Long Beach, Palmdale, and Ontario were small in comparison to LAX, so we might be able to cover Long Beach and Ontario on one day, Burbank and Palmdale the next day, and spend the rest of the week at LAX, where we would be close to the office so we could do both paperwork and airport work too. Our plan came together quickly, and we spent the rest of the afternoon reading the documents we had been given. Agent Stanton made several phone calls to each of the five airports we would be visiting in the next seven days, and made arrangements for airport consortium meetings to be held at each airport to discuss the security measures and observations that were required. Agent Stanton seemed to know key people at each of these airports and I was envious of his expertise and knowledge. But I had to admit I was catching up fast.

We didn't leave the office that night until 10:00, but we agreed to meet back at the office at 0600 the next morning. Agent Stanton had me sign out a G-car for our trip to Long Beach and Ontario Airports.

I arrived at the office at 0530 the next morning to find Agent Stanton having his second cup of coffee. He had arrived before me once again. It seemed he never went home. I filled my thermos with coffee and we headed for the G-car. We decided to head to Ontario Airport first since Agent Stanton had been able to arrange a meeting with the airport assistant director and most of the airlines station managers for 0800. We calculated that we should be able to drive the sixty-five miles to the airport and arrive before the 8:00 meeting. We had the benefit of using the carpool lane since there were two of us in the vehicle. We didn't have any special privileges, no fancy flashing lights, like law enforcement or the FBI on any federal, state, or local highway, so we obeyed all of the driving requirements just as normal drivers did. We also drove with greater care, watching our speed, for our car's license plates indicated we worked for the government, and we didn't want to break any laws.

We arrived at Ontario Airport at 0730. We parked in the designated government vehicle parking spot, which was near the main terminal. The law enforcement/safety office there had graciously given us one of their parking spots so we didn't have to park in the main parking lot and walk any distance to the terminal area. We were especially appreciative this morning since the jet stream had dropped unusually low into the lower part of the United States from Canada and Alaska, and it was mighty chilly and windy outside. We figured the winds were gusting to about forty-five miles per hour, and the outside air temperature was 47 degrees. It was bone-chilling cold for this time of year.

When we arrived at the airport manager's office at 0745, many of the managers that we wanted to speak with were already there. Agent Stanton knew all of the airline station managers and the airport managers, so he introduced me to everyone before the meeting started.

The meeting began promptly at 0800 hours and the Ontario Airport Assistant Station Manager, Roger Finn, welcomed everyone and said that this meeting was held at the request of the FAA, so without further ado he introduced Agent Stanton.

Agent Stanton stood tall before this group of mostly middle-aged and older men. Most of the airline station managers here had been with their designated airlines over twenty years, and were well-seasoned in every facet of the aviation industry. I later learned that Ontario was a coveted airport for airline employees because it was surrounded by a low cost of living area; the airport property was enormous so there was plenty of room for expansion, which meant potentially more jobs, and the airport itself was easy to navigate around, which made it a very pleasant place to work. It was not nearly as crowded or hectic as LAX, so it had a very comfortable and down-home feeling. Everyone knew one another, worked well together, and often got together for social events.

Before Agent Stanton began discussing the purpose of this meeting, he thanked everyone for agreeing to meet on such short notice, and then he had me stand so he could introduce me to everyone. Everyone in the conference room murmured hello and then looked curiously back at Stanton.

The explanation for the meeting started with the background information. Most of the people in this room were very aware of the crashes, but it was always good to explain why the pending security changes were happening, because it sometimes defused frustrated managers who didn't want to spend more money than originally anticipated in their annual budget, redirect staffing, or put additional requirements on passengers, who sometimes saw security as a impediment to their traveling ease and comfort.

Next, Stanton explained that he and I would be conducting tests, along with certifying that all of the equipment we tested was FAA certified and approved for continued use. This was going to be done on all of the walk-through metal detectors and x-ray machines today and tomorrow, and he also asked for an airline security representative to accompany us, as well as asking what would be the best time to conduct these tests so we could possibly work around any peak flight hours in an attempt to not inconvenience anyone.

Finally, he explained as Supervisor Drake did yesterday with us, the second phase of these security changes, which would be the most expensive and onerous to everyone, especially the airport operations department that was responsible for the badging office.

You could have heard a pin drop while this briefing was being given. Agent Stanton spoke for about twenty minutes before he stopped and asked if anyone had any questions. And all at once, as if the room had erupted, everyone began speaking at once. Agent Stanton looked around the entire room, pretty much unfazed by all of the commotion, and with precision and a full command of presence, he began pointing at one person at a time while calling out their name. The room began quieting down as each station manager asked their questions, some voicing their complaints.

In reality, everyone in the room knew that the FAA was the 800-pound gorilla, and what the FAA said was the final say, but Agent Stanton did an excellent job of listening to and answering every question until there were no more questions. I was taking notes fast and furiously in case we needed to report any of our conversations over the next few days to either a supervisor or someone above him. It seemed like the logical thing to do even though no one asked. Sometimes you just did what made sense and hoped for the best. As I scribbled away, I thought, *Better too much information than not enough.*

When the meeting was just about to be concluded, one of the station managers introduced us to Fred Myers, who would be assisting us with phase one of our visit there, working with all of the airport security equipment. Agent Stanton shook Fred's hand, as did I.

After picking up three cups of coffee, we sat down in a nearby passenger gate lounge area to decide on a game plan for our check-point equipment testing. We found out from Fred that Ontario Airport had fifteen walk-through metal detectors and five x-ray machines to test and certify. The best time to conduct the testing without passengers being present would be between 2100 hours in the evening and 0500 hours in the morning. Agent Stanton and I looked at one another, already knowing what the answer would be, and I asked Fred if he would be available to meet us tonight so we could do the testing during off hours. Fred said he thought he could, but would need to confirm it with his manager and would get back to us as soon as possible.

When Fred left to go find his manager we decided to walk through the terminal; for me it was my first visit to this airport, and Agent Stanton hadn't been there in a few months. So it was good to walk and talk and see where all of the equipment was located in preparation for our visit later that evening.

A few minutes later, Fred found us and said that he was authorized to work overtime, so we set up a place and time to meet later that evening. We said our farewells until later, and headed back to our G-car for the drive to Long Beach Airport, where Agent Stanton had scheduled a meeting for 1400 hours.

We arrived at Long Beach Airport in plenty of time for our meeting and parked in the main parking lot, which was directly across from the small terminal. The airport manager's office was upstairs above the main terminal, so we climbed the windy staircase up to his office located on the second floor. Long Beach Airport was a historic airport, so most of the terminal area had not been changed or modified in any way for many years, since it was protected under the California Historic Society Act. I was glad that it was protected and had stayed virtually the same all these years.

When I was a little girl, my sister, brother, and I would fly from Long Beach to San Francisco a few times a year to visit our mom. After my parents divorced, my mom moved back to the San Francisco area, where her mother lived, to get back on her feet and figure out what her next game plan in life was going to be. I didn't understand any of the friction between my parents back then; I just knew that I loved getting on airplanes, and being seated by a window toward the front so I could watch the ground passing quickly beneath my feet, floating in and out of clouds, some flights with bumpy rides, some just whispers of white and gray passing smoothly, silently, and effortlessly by us. To me it was magic, and I knew from the time I first stepped onto an airplane that somehow, someway, someday I was going to be involved in aviation.

I had never been upstairs from the main terminal area, back behind the scenes of this antique and lovely airport, so I was intrigued from the minute I stepped on the first stair.

The meeting at Long Beach Airport ran pretty much like the one at Ontario, except with far fewer questions and fewer airline station managers in attendance. The airport had only one checkpoint. Five airlines were operating from Daugherty Field, but the station manager for American Airlines advised us that we would be able to test the equipment immediately after this meeting, since there was a lull between the afternoon flights and the last few flights for the evening. One of his ticket agents could provide us with any other additional information that we needed.

The second phase, for badging, was going to take minimal time to complete, and everyone was in agreement that even though Long Beach was a smaller airport, it was still part of the overall aviation community and needed the same level of protection that the rest of the regulated airports in the country had.

When the meeting came to a close we walked back downstairs, stepping on the mosaic pattern sun design that was brightly embedded in the tile on the landing between the second and first floors. We walked past walls with probably fifty old photos of what the airport used to look like. Plaques hung telling the story of Earl S. Daugherty, a famous aviator, who in 1924 convinced the city council of Long Beach to begin the process of converting eighty acres of land owned by the Water Department into the beginnings of the Long Beach

Municipal Airport. From that time forward and into the 1960s, the airport grew in size and modernization. Today, Long Beach remains relatively unchanged except for the type of aircraft and the clothing the pilots, flight attendants, and passengers wear. These halls were a walk down memory lane and a delight to see. I was very pleased that someone who loved aviation so much had kept, and now displayed, all these old photos of flying days gone by.

At the checkpoint, Agent Stanton and I met with an airline representative and we began matching the paperwork with the actual name and serial number for the equipment at the checkpoint. We conducted our tests by either walking through the walk-through metal detector with various forbidden items on our person, or placing a forbidden item in an empty briefcase to see if the machines alarmed appropriately or the images appeared on the x-ray monitor. We recorded all of our findings on the documentation that was provided to us by Washington, DC.

At the conclusion of our testing we advised the airport manager that our testing protocol was complete, the equipment was fully functional, and that the FAA was certifying the equipment. We said our goodbyes and let him know we were leaving the airport and heading out to Ontario Airport. We again shook hands all around and headed back to our G-car.

We had finished up at Long Beach at 6:00 p.m., and planned to meet Fred at Ontario Airport at 8:30 p.m., so we had two and a half hours to grab something to eat, fuel the car, and drive back from the 405 freeway, to the 605, to the 10 freeway east toward Ontario. It was another sixty-five miles of multiple freeways, but we felt the traffic would be lighter since it was getting late and the normal commute traffic would already be off the freeways, cars nestled in their driveways or garages, resting their tires until the next day when they repeated their driving cycle once again.

We fueled the car, grabbed some Taco Bell for dinner, and headed back toward Ontario. Agent Stanton phoned his wife while we were waiting for our food to see how her day went and to say hello to his kids, since he was going to miss their bedtimes again tonight. He hung up his phone and turned with a smile. "They understand; I have one terrific family." I smiled back while sadly thinking that I didn't have anyone to call. I thought back to Marana and my last conversation with Jerry. *What a chump he was. He hurt everyone, but most of all he hurt his family,* I thought to myself.

Luckily the traffic was very light, and we arrived back at Ontario Airport just a little after 8:00 p.m. We met Fred at the appointed time and place. We knew it was going to be a long evening because we had twenty pieces of security equipment that needed to be checked and then certified as operational.

We began our testing and certification process at 2000 hours, and we finished at 0200 hours. One machine that was used as a secondary screening machine was the only piece of equipment that did not pass. It was immediately taken out of service and Fred said he would ensure that if any secondary screening was needed at that particular checkpoint, only hand wands or pat-downs would be authorized. I could see Agent Stanton making a mental note of that, and I of course wrote it down, for I had the feeling that sometime later this week we would be re-visiting Ontario Airport to ensure that those alternative procedures had been implemented.

We arrived back at the field office at 0300 hours and agreed to meet the next morning at 0900 hours. We would write up our field notes for Ontario and Long Beach so that information could be given to the regional office as quickly as possible, and set up our meeting at Palmdale Airport for 1500 hours.

I think as soon as I unlocked my apartment door and kicked my shoes off I was already sleep-walking toward my bed. I tumbled in without even getting undressed. I was exhausted, but in a good way. I knew that Agent Stanton and I had gotten a great deal done in the past twenty-four hours. We were organized, systematic, and thorough. I was learning by doing, which was my favorite way to learn.

As soon as the alarm went off, I got up, turned on the coffee pot and put on my running clothes to take a very short run down to the grocery store and back, knowing that I was out of half and half. The half-mile run to the store and the return trip would not only allow me to have a great cup of coffee, but would be just enough of a stretch to wake me up and get my circulation moving. I knew today and the rest of the week would require extremely long days, and this might be my only chance for a run this week. "Come on lazy bones, get going," I said while lacing up my shoes for my short run to the store and back.

When I got back I poured a cup of coffee while I was getting ready for work, and got my thermos out to take my second cup with me. I was dressed and out the door by 0830 and at the office easily by 0900 hours.

I walked into a nearly empty office, except for Stanton and Drake, who were standing by the coffee machine in the kitchen, deep in conversation. I could see Cindy in her office working away on her computer as she sat behind her desk with her chair swiveled around so her back was facing the door.

Walking over to my desk, I passed Kelly, said good morning, and asked how everything was going. She smiled saying she was busy beyond belief but was happy to assist in any way she could. She said the e-mails had slowed down from the regional office, so it seemed like everything was going along as planned. "Well, that's good," I said. I went and sat at my desk, turned on my computer, and began organizing the paperwork that Agent Stanton and I had compiled yesterday. We wanted to get our reports to Drake and the regional office as soon as we could before we moved on to another airport, so when we wrote our reports the information would be fresh in our minds.

After several hours of working on reports, it was time to head north toward Palmdale. Palmdale didn't have any commercial flights at the time, but they flew several government contract flights per week and had checkpoint screening equipment, so we were required to test and certify it. It would take us about two hours to get to Palmdale up in the high desert above Los Angeles off of Interstate 5. We knew the traffic would be light at this time of morning, so getting through the Sepulveda Pass and out of Los Angeles would be fairly easy.

When we arrived at Palmdale, we weren't exactly sure where to park since neither one of us had been to this airport before. The airport property was enormous, similar to Ontario Airport, with miles of fence line enclosing flat and barren land with only a few buildings and a long airstrip placed in the middle. However, we managed just fine and found the airport manager's office just inside the small terminal. As we walked toward his office, we could see the checkpoint and noted that there was one x-ray machine and one walk-through. "If all goes well, this should be fairly simple," Agent Stanton said to me. I nodded my head in agreement.

It proved to be fairly simple. The airport manager and his operations director were attentive, asked very few questions, and fully understood the purpose of our visit. At the end of our meeting, which lasted about thirty minutes, we walked over to the security checkpoint to conduct our testing and certification process. We finished up and were able to get back on the road by 5:00 p.m. Fortunately for us, the traffic was heavy in the opposite direction so we arrived back at the office in about an hour and a half. We wrote up our report for Palmdale and by 2000 hours we were headed out the door agreeing to be back at the office at 0600 so we could get out to Burbank Airport.

As we drove to Burbank Airport the following morning, it was hard to believe that it was only Tuesday. We had pretty much been working nonstop since Sunday, so the days and hours were running together by this point. The schedule was grueling, but we were on track and meeting the timelines that we had established for ourselves.

Burbank had three checkpoints and multiple air carriers that flew out of the tiny airport tucked away off the 101 freeway in Burbank. Burbank was a high-profile airport, in that many celebrities and businessmen flew in and out of Burbank due to its close proximity to Hollywood and the neighboring million-dollar homes nearby. We didn't want to disrupt the checkpoints, but we knew that we had to get this airport finished up today because we would need the rest of the week at LAX. The airline station managers helped us immensely by giving us the flight time schedules, enabling us to work around peak flight hours. Fortunately there were enough breaks during the day and early evening that we finished up at 2200 hours and were on the road and heading back to the office. Another long day, but the mission was accomplished.

Once again at 0600 hours the next morning, we arrived at the office and wrote our report for Burbank. After we hit the send button a few hours later, we began discussing our plan for LAX Airport.

LAX would be the biggest work load yet, since there are eight terminals at LAX with multiple airlines. Our meeting with the airport was scheduled for 1300 hours, so we had some time to discuss ideas on how to try to do most of the checkpoint testing at night after most of the flights had already departed.

The meeting with the managers at the LAX Airport went very well, although longer than anticipated because of the number of questions that were asked by airport officials — both the domestic and foreign airline station managers. But by then Agent Stanton and I were seasoned at giving these types of briefings, and between the two of us we were able to succinctly answer every question. During the meeting we identified which checkpoints we could test during daylight hours, and which ones we would test after all of the flights had departed. A plan was mapped out with which everyone was in agreement.

Wednesday and Thursday flew by, and before we knew it, Friday was knocking at our door, with a deadline due. Fortunately for us, we had written our reports after the completion of each airport testing and certification, so we only had to get the report turned in for LAX. Some of the other agents had planned out their schedules differently, and you could tell that the scramble was on to meet the deadline. The office was buzzing with the clicking of keys on everyone's computers and the chatter back and forth between all of the agents. The pit was full of activity that day and I am sure the orange carpet in the office gained a few more coffee stains as a badge of proof that the work was getting done.

We left the office Friday at 1800 hours, confident and elated that we had met an extremely difficult timeline. I caught up with Kelly as she was heading toward her car. She said some of her friends were heading down to Rivera in Redondo Beach for a beer and wanted to know if I'd like to join them. I said, "Yes indeed, I would like that very much; a glass of wine seems like a pretty good idea after this week's hectic schedule." I lived two blocks from Hennessey's where everyone was meeting, so I drove home, parked my car in my garage, grabbed my mail, looking quickly at it before throwing it on the table, closed the back door, and walked over to Hennessey's where everyone was already gathering and chatting away about the week.

On Monday I arrived at the office at 0545, and for the first time managed to get into the office before Agent Stanton. I was sitting at my desk trying to piece together my time card for Kelly. In order for me to get paid correctly, Kelly would be inputting our work hours into the Consolidated Automated System for Time and Labor Entry (CASTLE). She would be inputting the data for Agent Stanton too. When he arrived at the office, he sat down and began collecting his time card information. Everything needed to be reviewed and approved by Supervisor Drake before it was given to Kelly to input. All of this needed to be accomplished by the end of the day every other Wednesday, so it was best to get it all in early.

After we got our time cards completed and turned in, Agent Stanton and I began mapping out a plan for the oversight Phase 2, the airport identification badging reconciliation that had already begun at each of the sixteen airports in our region, along with the rest in the country. The airport operator had a three-month window to complete this audit and rebadging, which seemed like a long time, but when you think of airports like LAX that have almost 50,000 employees, it's like taking a small city and having the city hall employees issue a new badge to every single citizen in their city. The task was enormous, time-consuming, and expensive for the airport operators. And the FAA was not providing any funding, just the mandate that the new procedures be in place by the end of April.

For the next three months, Agent Stanton and I traveled between

LAX, Burbank, Palmdale, Long Beach, and Ontario Airports observing, discussing, and suggesting ways to accomplish this change in airport security measures. Fortunately, four out of the five airports were all managed by the Los Angeles Airport Authority, so funding or staffing wasn't as much of a problem as it was at other airports. Burbank had to implement the security measures on their own, like most of the other airports, but the networking that had been created over the years helped everyone.

For me personally, in January 1989, a milestone had been reached when I found the personnel action, Standard Form 50 (SF-50) that I had completed my first year of federal service and was officially off probation. My first year of employment with the FAA made me feel like I was fireproof, waterproof, and bulletproof; after all, they didn't call me "Mad Dog Stewart" for nothing! When I told Agent Stanton that I was off probation, he bellowed out his hearty congratulations and offered to buy me a cup of coffee. "Now that's a partner!" and we walked over to the coffee pot, mugs in hand, and he poured me a slightly stale cup of thick black coffee. With great ceremony he dropped a quarter into the coffee jar and we went back to our desks.

By the time April 30th arrived, I had gotten used to 65-hour work weeks; I could almost close my eyes and drive to the office in my sleep. Between January and April the special agents and staff at the Los Angeles Field Office had assisted in significant security changes in the aviation community that became permanent fixtures for every airline and airport across America.

It was quitting time, and I was looking forward to the first full weekend off in months. The weather was beginning to warm up and I thought I might be able to get out on the water and kayak on Saturday. A few months ago I had found a sit-on-top kayak at a garage sale: kayak, seat, and paddle all for $75. I couldn't turn it down. The yellow kayak was scuffed and dirty, but sound, so I bought it. After a good scrubbing it looked pretty darn good, in my opinion, and I was more than ready to get out on the water. *King Harbor, here I come this weekend*, I thought.

After clearing off my desk and securing all of my files for the weekend, I started to walk over to Agent Stanton's desk to say good night and that I'd see him on Monday.

Just as I arrived in front of Stanton's desk, Supervisor Drake hollered from his office door, "Stewart, pack your bags, you're going to Brussels."

CHAPTER SEVEN

Traveling in Teams

"BRUSSELS?" I SAID as I put my gear back on my desk and headed toward Drake's office.

"Yep — plan on leaving here in ten days. Now, that you've got all of the security measures in place at your airports, it's time to go help the teams that are in Europe. So, when you come back to work on Monday, Kelly will begin helping you with your travel plans. There will be several of you going."

Supervisor Drake continued, "A few months ago headquarters implemented additional security measures overseas as a result of Pan Am 103. We've all been busy stateside because of PSA 1771, but now the agents in Europe need some extra hands. If you think we're stretched thin, you should see staffing levels there. Anyway, they need some assistance and you, Big Earl, and Rob are going from this office. Now, get outta here, have a good weekend, and I'll see you on Monday. I'll explain more to everyone next week."

I grabbed my stuff off my desk and sprinted out the door. "YES! I'm going to Brussels," I excitedly said to no one in particular.

Early Saturday morning, I decided to put my scruffy yellow kayak in my Jeep and head over to King Harbor to go for a paddle. I shoved the 45-pound Neoprene compound-shaped kayak on the top of my Jeep, tied her down, and headed out. I knew just where to launch since I had scoped everything out, actually stumbling on the launch area when I was out for a run and was trying to stay as close to the water as I could, just to avoid running along the busy streets of Redondo and Hermosa.

I drove the short distance to the dock to find the early-morning outrigger canoe team just launching their slick canoes into the chilly water. These guys and gals were serious racers and I admired their strength and stamina. I had a lot of strength and stamina too, but I liked paddling alone because I enjoyed the solitude, peace, and quiet. I also gained clarity when kayaking or running alone. I needed my quiet time to get my thoughts in order. Kayaking is so much different from running, in that you get immediate solace; as compared to running, you feel a totally different kind of peace and quiet. You're always talking in your head when you run, mapping out a plan. When you're on the water, you become one with the water. Sounds kind of kooky, but for me that's exactly what happens.

I waited until the outriggers were well away from the dock before I launched. I kept my lightweight water shoes on, which immediately got wet along with my rump. "Brr," escaped my lips as I settled into the seat sitting on top of the kayak. Yes indeed, the water was chilly, but it was worth it. I pushed away from the dock and began the two-stroke paddle from side to side as I paddled away toward the harbor. I planned to paddle inside the harbor first and get comfortable with the kayak and my stroke. As I paddled, water dripped onto my lap, so I knew I was pretty much going to be wet from the waist down by the time I was finished, but I didn't care. I was on the water, which was exactly what I needed to be doing. I wore a rubberized zip-up jacket designed for paddlers, and a hat, so my upper body and core stayed warm.

It was a picture-perfect day to be on the water. The water was still cold, but the May air was bringing warmth to the sea breeze as summer approached. The brown pelicans and various types of gulls barely moved as I paddled by. It seems creatures and men are at peace with one another when they are on the water. It's a respect and partnership shared in this salty body of water that is two-thirds our planet. I wished this tranquility could be transferred to the remaining third of our planet. I paddled on into the morning, feeling the strain of unused muscles, saying good morning to a few fellow paddlers out on the water, and the boaters who were either working on their boats or sitting on them and enjoying a morning cup of hot coffee.

When I got back to the dock, the tide had come in, which made the dock partly submerged underwater. Docks normally float, so being submerged usually isn't a problem, but this particular dock didn't seem to float very well, so it was constantly at the mercy of the tides. I was at the mercy of the tides right now too, but fortunately for me, I had water shoes on so I was able to maneuver my kayak onto the dock pretty easily. I dragged and carried the kayak back to my Jeep, but I was tired from the two-hour paddle, and hungry, too!

When I got home, my neighbors were both coming out of their apartments at the same time. Two single guys, both named Bill, but totally different both in looks and personalities. I could tell by the way they dressed that one Bill was very neat and organized, and the other Bill was more of a dreamer and didn't worry about dress or being organized, I suspected. On several occasions I would hear the not-so-organized Bill say "shoot," followed by footsteps stomping up the short flight of stairs to retrieve whatever he had forgotten. It was comical and I always chuckled when I heard Bill mumbling away to himself.

"Hi, how are you? Beautiful day isn't it?" I said to the two of them. They both bobbed their heads, while waving, and headed off in different directions.

Bill and Bill lived in the two apartments that were upstairs above the garages. They had ocean views but they had told me their rents were less than mine because they both had been there ten-plus years and their apartments weren't remodeled, whereas mine was completely remodeled. I was the first tenant to enjoy the beauty of this tiny remodeled beach cottage. There were only four units, two downstairs at the front of the lot closest to the street, and two upstairs over the garages in the back of the lot. There was a big open area between the front and back units, and four garages underneath the upstairs apartments. Everyone had their own one-car garage. The unit next to me was still empty because it was getting remodeled, like mine. It was nice to have great neighbors, and I felt like I had found a secret treasure in the midst of a big city. Close to the beach, work, and all the necessities of living: a dream life, a dream job; I was a happy woman.

I also had found the perfect church for me. On Massy Street in Hermosa Beach was the smallest of the three Catholic churches in the area. The priest from time to time would refer Our Lady of Guadalupe as the "little one" because it was between the two larger churches of St. James in Redondo Beach and American Martyrs in Manhattan Beach. There was something about this little church: a peace, a presence, a place of joy. I smiled or cried for joy every time I came to Mass here. I always felt like I was home. I usually went to 11:00 Mass on Sundays. That way I could sleep in!

The weekend flew by and I was looking forward to hearing all of the details about my first international trip as a special agent.

How or why it got stuck in my head, I don't know, but on the way to work I was humming The Mamas & The Papas "Monday, Monday," which was this band's only number one hit in the United States. Their other songs like "California Dreamin" and "If You can Believe Your Eyes and Ears" were big hits too, but "Monday, Monday" hit it out of the ball park. I listened to country music most of the time, so I wasn't even sure how I knew this song, but I guess it popped into my head because it was Monday. I just hoped it wouldn't be in my head all day.

The morning passed with a flurry of report-writing and case review. When an agent opens a potential violation against an air carrier or an airport, each case is identified with an EIR, or Enforcement Investigation Report number. The report has identification numbers and letters for the office that opened the case, plus the year and the sequential order number. Identifying a potential violation was determined by measuring the required regulations against the practices or procedures of the party responsible for adhering to the regulation, so for the most part, this was pretty straightforward work. Opening an investigation had a protocol: potential violation was discussed with our supervisor, and if they concurred, we drew an EIR number from the automated data system we had. A letter was sent out to the potential violator, briefing detailing the violation, and giving them the opportunity to respond within a certain period of time.

Some of these cases were generated by the agents themselves, and others were assigned to us by our supervisor. For instance, when a passenger carries an item either in their checked luggage or carry-on that is prohibited by the FAA, and the screening process that bag is subjected to finds the item, the airline notifies the FAA. A letter of investigation is sent to the passenger and they are given an opportunity to respond. An EIR number for the case is pulled from the data system and that case is assigned to one of the special agents in the office, usually to the agent that is responsible for the airport.

Each field office has a number of airports within their geographical jurisdiction that they are responsible for. Any security incident, airline, airport, individual, or passenger will be investigated by the agent assigned to that airport, and most likely, the case that is opened will be handled by the agent in charge. Logic says the bigger the airport the greater the probability of more cases being opened because of passenger capacity and the number of airlines operating from that airport.

The flurry of report-writing involving writing investigative reports is based on the facts discovered by the special agent in conjunction with their duties, and what the alleged violator said when they responded to the letter of investigation that was sent to them. Once an EIR was opened, the case had to be presented to your manager and then be ready for their signature within thirty days. Needless to say, if you had multiple cases to write, you were going to be busy. And in most cases overtime was not authorized for paperwork.

I wasn't behind schedule yet, but I was getting close. Between my first air marshal mission, training in Oklahoma City, and the additional security measures as a result of PSA 1771, I had a pile of cases to compete over the next couple of weeks before I went on travel again.

For the next ten days, my computer and I bonded with every key stroke. While rubbing my neck, I swore silently to myself, saying, "Come on, Maggie — keep going, girl. You've got to get these cases done." My neck and shoulders took the brunt of the load, but I kept at it.

With a few days to spare, I managed to get ten passenger cases, one airport, and three air carrier cases completed. "Wow, Maggie — way to go, girl!" I said out loud to no one in particular. As I placed the completed cases in Drake's in-box, I thought, *Supervisor Drake's going to be smiling today for a change.*

Those few days to spare would afford Supervisor Drake time to read, review, and return any cases to me for correction. And I usually did get some cases returned for various writing style changes, grammar, and a few technical errors. But this was a necessary and critical process, for when these cases left our office and went to the regional office for a second level of review, they were expected to be perfect. When those cases were reviewed and signed off by the regional office, they then went to the legal department in the region for local civil penalty action.

Once these cases were received and accepted by legal, their office notified the violator of the civil penalty amount that would be levied on them and the violator could either pay the amount or ask for an administrative hearing to further state their case. In some cases, we were called in as subject-matter experts to testify why the violation occurred and our reasoning for the civil penalty. This didn't happen very often, but the case needed to be air tight in case it did.

In the meantime, Kelly had once again assisted Big Earl, Rob, and me with our travel arrangements to Brussels, along with confirming our hotel reservations. We'd all be traveling on Sunday so we could arrive in Brussels for our briefings the following Tuesday. For all of her hard work, I'd have to try and remember to bring her something back, I thought to myself as I headed out the door to pack once again.

LAX Airport and I were becoming the best of friends, between my being one of the agents assigned to the airport along with fourteen of the fifty-four air carriers that operated out of LAX, along with all of my travel.

"I'm back," I said with a smile on my face as I walked into the American Airlines terminal.

I was really beginning to know the ropes of the airport, and found that once you understood the layout, it wasn't such a complicated airport after all. My dad, when he was alive, used to complain about LAX all the time, and if he ever had to travel, he would make sure he went out of Long Beach or even John Wayne Airport in Orange County. I've met a lot of people since that complain about LAX too, but I was getting used to the layout and actually enjoyed all the hustle and bustle.

I boarded the American Airlines flight to JFK New York at 0600 hours for the five and a half hour flight to New York, where I would change flights, boarding another American Airlines flight at 1810 hours for the seven hour and forty-five minute flight to Brussels. It was going to be a brutal day with such a long trip ahead, but I had brought several books with me and knew I had time to read them, for I wasn't in air marshal capacity on this trip. I was a passenger just like everyone else, sitting in an aisle seat and people-watching as every-one boarded and placed their carry-on luggage in the overhead bins, or somewhere else if their bin was full. The B-747 was being boarded from the rear of the aircraft forward, so it was orderly. The passengers were varied, from children to elderly. Summer vacation had already begun for some families, as could be seen by the excitement in both the children and parents' eyes as they boarded the aircraft for New York. A large group of teenagers boarded and were seated us just a few rows in front of me and I wondered who they were — school band, summer camp, or some other interesting group trip. *Fun times ahead for them*, I thought to myself.

Again, this flight went quickly, and many of the passengers slept for a portion of the way since it had departed so early in the morning.

We arrived at JFK on time, and I deplaned and headed toward my next gate. I had over three hours before my next flight departed, so I had plenty of time to get something to eat and people-watch.

I hadn't spent much time at JFK — or in New York, for that matter. I had been there only one other time, when I was much younger. The airport was teeming with people of every color, shape, and dress. People hustled around at a frantic pace as if every minute was all that mattered, and they must get to where they were going.

The normal personal space separation that comes so naturally to Americans was lost in the tide of nationalities as people bumped into one another, running their carry-on bags over the tops of people's shoes. Feet that were moving too slowly or standing in the way got run over with complete disregard for common courtesy. Yet somehow, it was all right. That's just how it is in New York; the pace is maddening.

After several hours of walking and watching people, it was again time for me to board the American Airlines flight for my flight to Brussels. I hadn't seen Big Earl or Rob and of course, I had forgotten to ask them what their flight schedules were before I left the office on Friday. I knew I would see them Monday afternoon at the Civil Aviation Security Office in Brussels, so I wasn't too worried. I couldn't check into my hotel until 3:00, so I wasn't sure what I was going to do all morning, not only with my luggage, but my struggle to stay awake! Jet lag was going to be with me once again for a few days, I suspected.

Just as I thought, after we landed in Brussels, I felt as if I had been run over by a Mack truck. I didn't sleep much on the flight over, so my eyes were bloodshot, tired, dry, irritated, and I had the beginnings of dark circles under my eyes. I knew sunshine and a walk were going to do me good when I got out of the airport and to my hotel.

I arrived by cab at the hotel, which was a few short blocks from the office. It was true that I could not check in until 3:00 p.m., but the desk clerk showed me where I could leave my luggage and gave me a tag so I could claim it upon my return. Just as I was leaving the bag room, Big Earl and Rob arrived at the hotel. The two of them looked as bad as I felt and we laughed at the sight of one another. I waited for them to drop their bags at the bag room so the three of us could find something to eat. "You boys got to know me by now; I'm always hungry," I said. They looked at me, smiled, and nodded in agreement.

The three of us decided to grab a bite to eat, and started finding our way to the office. The front desk clerk had given us directions for the short four-block walk to the American Embassy, where our security office was located. The clerk had also told us to try the waffles, or gauffres as they were called here, that were sold at local street stands throughout the city. We thanked her and headed off on our way. Walking with the sun shining on my face revived me enough to know that I was hungry and was looking forward to that waffle. We stopped at the first stand we found, ordered five waffles, two each for the guys and one for me, along with three Cokes. As we walked and ate, we commented that the waffles were indeed delicious. And then to our sheer delight, we came around a corner and began walking toward the Grand Place.

We discovered later that the Grand Place started off as a market for trading goods. Initially wooden houses were scattered around the market, but by the fourteenth century, they had been replaced by stone mansions. The town hall has a tower 96 meters high, with a metal statue of the Archangel Michael, the patron saint of Brussels, slaying a dragon or devil on top. The Grand Place was bombed in 1695 by the French, but the damaged town hall was reconstructed. The square was teeming with people; tourists and busy locals either getting a bite to eat, shopping, or passing through on the way to another destination, as were we. The old buildings were beautiful — a Gothic style that I had never seen before. I would have wandered this square for hours, looking at every stone, design, and building if I could have. Alas, we had a very important meeting to get to.

We arrived at the American Embassy with our passports in hand and explained what the purpose of our visit was. The guard on duty had a guest list already at his duty station and he was able to grant us access to the embassy after we signed in, and with his help, wrote down the office and room number we were going to. I was glad we had left in plenty of time, because I didn't anticipate this extra level of security. I assumed we were going to a regular office building. Pan Am 103 had stolen the innocence from the world, and now security was tighter overseas than in America, even though America was catching up fast. "Be sure to always plan for additional time when attending meetings in foreign countries," I said to myself as I cleared security.

We located the office on the fifth floor and the secretary directed us to another office on the third floor, which actually turned out to be a small auditorium that seated about fifty people. There were several people already there. I quickly scanned the room, but didn't know anyone. One of the people in the room told us there was a sign-in sheet up front for everyone to sign in.

After signing in, I said hello to several people I passed as I went and found an aisle seat about five rows from the front. I wanted to be close enough to see what was going on, but like in church, not in the front row. Earl and Rob sat down near me, too. Fortunately we were fifteen minutes early, so we had time to relax and collect our thoughts. I had brought a notepad with me in case we could take notes. For the next fifteen minutes people wandered in, signed in, looked around, and found seats. By the time everyone was seated, it looked as if every seat was taken.

At 1300 hours, a gentleman who had been seated in the front row stood up, turned around, and asked if everyone could hear him. The acoustics in the auditorium were excellent; his voice could be heard loud and clear throughout the room. He introduced himself as Tom and then turned and pointed to two other people and introduced them.

Tom stated the obvious by saying, "Good afternoon. As you all know, you have been sent here to assist our office with conducting air carrier inspections on the US Airlines that are operating out of Europe, heading to the United States. Since the bombing of Pan Am 103, additional security measures have been implemented on flights to and from the United States. But because there are so many flights and so few special agents to inspect, a 'special assessment' had been called by Washington, DC. Each one of us was the additional assistance that the foreign assessment team needed."

Tom further explained that this was the first effort of this magnitude and that he was the team coordinator for this two-week assessment. Everyone in the room would be teamed up with another special agent, and we would be deployed to a specific location to conduct air carrier assessments. The teams would depart here on Wednesday, so tomorrow, Tuesday, would be spent getting over jet lag, and reviewing the assessment protocol with our team member.

"Flight and hotel arrangements have been made so when your names are called, Sally, our administrative assistant, will give you each a packet containing your travel documents. The first name I call will be the team leader and the second name I call will be a team member. We recognize that many of you are new to aviation security, so we paired you up with a senior agent to not only provide some level of expertise, but continuity throughout the teams and the assessment process. Standardization is important for this assessment," Tom stated in a matter-of-fact tone.

Continuing on, Tom said, "Once you get your packets you'll notice that you will return here prior to heading back to the States and spend a couple of days writing up your findings and your reports. The format is standardized, and the special agents based here in Brussels will help you with your report-writing when you return. The goal is to have all of the reports written and submitted to Washington, DC prior to your leaving. We all know how busy everyone is at home and we don't want this put on a back burner after you leave Europe. The information you provide us will be used as direct feedback to measure the security posture of the airlines operating in and out of Europe, and it will assist the staff in DC greatly to understand what, if anything, needs to be revised.

"Are there any questions so far?" Tom asked. No one spoke. "Okay, I'll start calling out the teams now, and where you'll be going."

One by one Tom started calling out names and the destinations they were bound for. At one point Tom chuckled and said, "Remember, guys, there's no trading for the good destinations either."

My name was called in tandem with the name Ed Brown. An elderly gentleman stood up first, walked up and got his packet, and then walked back to his seat and sat down. I too went and got my packet and decided to go sit with Ed Brown. When I walked over to where he was sitting, he didn't so much as look at me. He just stared straight ahead with a look of discontentment on his face. I said hello and sat in the row behind him. *What am I in for now?* I wondered.

When the meeting ended, Ed Brown said to meet him in the hotel lobby tomorrow morning at 0900 hours, and then got up and left. Big Earl and Rob had been asked by their team leaders to stay behind, so it was up to me to find my way back to the hotel on my own. Big Earl was going to Paris, and Rob was going to Germany. Ed Brown and I had been selected to go to Stockholm, Sweden. I briefly looked at my packet before I left the embassy and saw that the flight time was only two hours and ten minutes. *A piece of cake compared to what I have flown in the last thirty-six hours,* I thought.

I decided to walk back through the Grand Place on my way back to the hotel and sight-see just a little bit more. It was such a magnificent place, and I wanted to be amongst the people who shopped and marveled at its beauty as much as I did. As I wandered in and out of the shops, I knew I was hungry again and decided to eat now because I suspected once I got back to the hotel and checked in, I was going to call it a day. I could feel the fatigue creeping up on me like a slow-moving tide moving up on the beach, slowing covering your feet as it slips along, quietly hiding more and more shoreline sand with each passing hour.

I found a small café with outside seating and waited to be shown to a table. Once I was seated, I was handed a menu that appeared to be meant for tourists, with colorful pictures of several entrées. I wanted something warm, since I'd been eating a lot of snack food the past couple of days. I saw a picture that looked like beef stew. Below the picture it said Vlaamse Stovery (beef stew cooked in beer), a house specialty. That sounded perfect, so when the waiter came to my table I pointed to the picture and ordered that plus a Coke. He gave me a quick nod and disappeared. Once that decision was made I was able to spend some time sitting in the mild sunshine and people-watching. As always, it was a favorite pastime of mine no matter where I went. Here I caught bits and pieces of languages that I could not understand, but realized that no matter where they were from, everyone pretty much looked the same whether walking hand in hand in love, hurrying to an appointment, or tourist shopping. Our facial expressions when doing similar things were the same.

Soon the waiter came back with my Coke, again nodded, smiled, and placed the Coke on my table along with a small basket of bread. When my stew arrived I was very hungry and happily ate the delicious meal too quickly, but my stomach was content when I was done. When the waiter presented my check I already had my wallet on the table, so he assisted me with the monies I needed to pay the bill and advised me in broken English that it wasn't necessary to leave a tip (but it would be appreciated). "Thank you," I said to him in English, left him a tip, and began walking back toward the hotel which I knew was just a few blocks away.

By the time I got back to the hotel, collected my bag, and presented myself at the front desk, I was the only one needing to be checked in, so the service was rapid — superb and efficient. I received my room key and was asked whether I needed of a wake-up call the next morning, or anything else. "Yes, please; I would like a wake-up call. Thank you," I said to the desk clerk.

Once in my room, I locked the door behind me, plopped my suitcase on one of the twin beds, and went to look out the window. I was on the fourth floor and facing another building that looked like an office building. I didn't mind, since I was dead on my feet anyway and I knew we'd be in this hotel only tonight and tomorrow night.

I showered, changed into my bed clothes, and by 7:00 was fast asleep. When the phone rang at 0630 the next morning, I woke up to answer the telephone, realizing I had barely moved, for my bed covers and sheets looked just about the same as when I crawled into bed last night.

I felt refreshed but still in need of a cup of strong coffee, and I knew I would have to go downstairs to find any. So I quickly cleaned up, leaving my room within fifteen minutes in search of coffee. "I can finish getting ready after my first cup of coffee," was always my motto when I stayed in hotels.

Just a few minutes before 0900, I was down in the lobby waiting for Agent Brown. He had just walked out of the hotel restaurant with two other men and was walking toward the elevators when he saw me. He said he was going up to his room and would be back in a few minutes. The wait turned out to be almost thirty minutes by the time he came back downstairs. He didn't seem in a hurry and he didn't seem thrilled at the prospect of having to work with me for the next two weeks.

Special Agent Ed Brown was from the Baltimore Field Office and he had been with the government for many years, transferring to FAA Security a few years ago. He told me he had less than five years to go and he hadn't expected to travel so much. He wasn't hired as an air marshal but as a special agent, responsible for airport and air carrier inspections that were supposed to be done near or around the Baltimore Airport. At least that's what he was told when he had accepted the position. It was summertime back in Baltimore, and he wanted to be home spending time with his wife, mowing the lawn, and cleaning his pool, not in a foreign country training some newbie. Needless to say, our briefing didn't last long, and he told me he'd see me at the airport on Wednesday. Our flight departed at 10:00 a.m., so I needed to be there at 8:00 a.m., and he said, "Don't be late."

Yikes, this is going to be one heck of a trip, if this is the attitude I get to deal with every day, I thought. To shake off the negativity, I decided after our brief meeting that what I needed was a good long run before I sat down to review some of the documents we had been provided with yesterday. I went back up to my room, changed into my running gear, and headed out toward the Grand Place once again.

I knew that if nothing else, I could run to and from there a few times, getting some miles in, along with a good workout. It was all flat terrain, so it was an easy run on a picture-perfect, beautiful day. I was totally spent when I got back to the hotel, for I had run for almost two hours. It was exactly what I needed.

I'm a creature of habit sometimes when it comes to food. I cook and eat to sustain myself. I like food, but I don't necessarily love food, so if I find something I like I tend to order it again. I ate at the hotel restaurant and ordered their beef stew, which was not nearly as good as the café I ate at yesterday, but it would get me through the evening, and I'd have a wonderful warm gauffre from the street stand at the corner before I headed off to the airport.

When I got back to my room I read for a while, and once again fell asleep in a hard and deep sleep that allowed me to be rested and refreshed when I woke the next morning.

At 0800 hours, I was waiting in the lobby of the hotel, sitting in one of the overstuffed, gaudy chairs so typical of hotel lobbies. Where I was sitting, I could see both the elevator, and the front double doors of the hotel. The lobby was teeming with activity as people checked out, greeted colleagues that were either guests themselves, or someone picking up a guest, to scurry them off to a business meeting somewhere in the city. As in airports, I enjoyed people-watching, but this morning I had one eye on the elevator as well. I was restless, partly still trying to recover from jet lag, and partly because the agent I was going to be spending the next few weeks with was aloof, and clearly wanted to be somewhere else. I, on the other hand, was chomping at the bit to dive into something new, and see what the international arena was all about.

I glanced at my watch and again at the elevator door. Agent Brown exited with his roller bag tagging along behind him, looking reluctant as a little kid having to step onto a school bus, alone, to attend his first day of kindergarten. I stood as he walked toward me, but he continued toward the entrance doors of the hotel. He signaled, with a slight nod of his head, a few gray hairs dipping gently above his brow line as he did so, that I was to meet him outside. When I got outside, a cab door was just being opened for him. I walked around to the other side of the cab, and a door was opened for me, as well.

The fifteen-minute ride to the airport was spent in silence, for the most part, except for Agent Brown asking if I had my passport and other documents provided during the briefing earlier this week. I said I did, and then it appeared there was nothing left to be said.

When we arrived at the airport, Agent Brown paid the fare, and we proceeded into the terminal area to board our Scandinavian Airlines flight to Stockholm. We both checked our luggage, and processed through the remaining security procedures quickly. Once we were beyond screening, we walked to a coffee stand, where we found several other agents getting their coffee. Agent Brown knew a couple of them and they happily engaged in rapid conversations about where they were going, and introductions were made all around for those of us who didn't know them. It was the most animated and energized conversation I had seen since meeting Agent Brown.

The boarding announcements commenced and Agent Brown and I headed for the departure gate. The flight attendant took our boarding passes just prior to our walking down the jetway and informed us that this was an "open" seating flight and to take any seat we wanted. When we boarded, Agent Brown took a window seat in a row where the aisle seat was already taken. *Well, Maggie Stewart, isn't this something?* I thought as I took an aisle seat two rows behind him. I pulled a paperback from my backpack and settled in to read for the next few hours.

After landing, retrieving our luggage, and clearing customs, we headed out into the bright sunlight to find a taxi for the ride to our hotel. Agent Brown told the cab driver what hotel we were going to in Stockholm, along with giving him a slip of paper with the address on it. Agent Brown and I both sat in the back, he on the driver's side, and I on the passenger's side. He was quiet and seemed lost in thought as we pulled away from the airport.

I too became lost in thought, as I looked out the window watching, and trying to get a better bearing on where we were heading, and which direction. I glanced over at Agent Brown; he was very quiet, and then I looked at him more closely. His skin had turned the slightest color of ash. I'd see that color skin before, and I knew it wasn't good. I gently reached over, touched him on the right shoulder, asking if he was all right. He barely moved his head. The muscles in his neck involuntarily twitched slightly to the right, so he could look at me, with dull blank eyes, a whisper of movement, as he shook his head from side to side, indicating that he was not all right. He could not speak, could barely move, and slumped down into the cushion of the seat.

I immediately reached over, tapped the cab driver on the shoulder, and said, "We having a medical emergency here, and could you get us to the nearest hospital ASAP?" The cab driver looked at me, looked in his rear view mirror at Agent Brown, made a call on his radio and hit the gas pedal at the same time. The race to save a life was on.

Team Member Down

THE CAB DRIVER instantly knew the urgency and raced down the highway at record speed. I was partially holding Agent Brown up so he wouldn't slump over in the seat completely, while trying to hang on to something myself, since I had unbuckled my seatbelt. It was pure luck, along with fast, furious, and skilled driving that got us to the emergency room entrance of the Karolinska University Hospital in land-record-speed time. When we stopped, the cab driver literally flew out of his car, and dashed for the emergency room doors. Within seconds, medical personnel were running toward the cab and got Agent Brown out and onto a gurney. I grabbed my backpack and quickly followed. I didn't speak Swedish so I didn't understand a whole lot that was going on, but I followed their hurried footsteps into the hospital. I followed the medical staff into the private room and watched as they urgently tended to Agent Brown. I stood off to the side and noted that the time on the wall clock was 1400 hours. Finally, one of the nurses saw me and said to come with her and she would show me where I could wait. She asked my name and relationship to Agent Brown. I gave her my name and explained that we worked together. She nodded, wrote my name down, and showed me where to wait.

The cab driver had been waiting for me outside in the hallway and when he saw me he asked in excellent English if the man from his cab was going to be all right. I said, "We're not sure yet, but I really appreciate your asking." I also asked what the fare was so I could pay him. He refused to accept any fare, gave me our luggage, and bid me farewell. I shook his hand, thanked him, and he turned and walked out of the hospital and into the bright sunlight – the bright sunlight that soon disappeared as those hospital doors ominously closed, leaving me trapped inside. Oh, how I wanted to escape and be outside feeling warmth and light, not dark and gloom.

"Get busy, pass the time, and be useful," I said out loud in the empty waiting room. I decided to start a log to capture the events of what was transpiring. I noted the time and worked backwards to determine the approximate time we had left the airport until now. Chronological order seemed logical, and knowing the government would immediately want an incident report once they found out what was going on, I decided to capture the events while they were fresh in my mind. There wasn't anyone in-country from our team to call, so I decided I needed to contact the US Embassy here in Stockholm and ask them to contact the embassy in Brussels for me. Once I got my notes in order, I walked to the nurses' station and asked if there was any update on Agent Brown, and if they could help me make a telephone call to the US Embassy. There was no update on Agent Brown, and the nurse said she would be more than happy to assist me.

The nurse picked up the telephone and called the hospital operator who, as I understood, was connecting her to the US Embassy. The only words I understood in the brief conversation were "American Embassy." The nurse spoke, waited, then spoke again for several minutes, and I am sure to various people, before she reached the correct office. It appeared all government agencies, even overseas, had to cut through ribbons of red tape before they found the right office and person to speak with. The nurse handed me the phone; I said "Thanks," and with a nod, she went back to work at her station.

"Hello, my name is Maggie Stewart and I need some assistance please," I said with a calm and collected voice.

"This is Jim Dryer, Resident Security Officer (RSO) for the embassy.

How can I help you?" he asked with a deep Southern accent.

I explained the medical situation, providing all the information that I knew, and that we were traveling on official business for the government. Jim Dryer listened intently, asked a few questions, and then said he would come over to the hospital immediately to assess the situation. He asked me to give the telephone back to the nurse so he could get the address and telephone number of the hospital. After handing the telephone back to the nurse and hearing the information exchanged, I went back to the waiting area.

I think I waited for about an hour before Jim Dryer walked into the waiting area. He was tall, thin, and looked like a runner; his brown hair was cropped military style; he had brown eyes, and a crooked nose that might have been from the result of a fight. I stood up and we both walked toward the center of the room and shook hands. I instantly felt a wave of relief because I knew someone could help me get in contact with the Brussels office so I could tell them what had happened.

Jim Dryer and I talked for several minutes. I looked at my log occasionally to make sure I had the times correct, because he was writing everything down on a notepad as we spoke. He then made a few phone calls on his cell phone, describing the situation to some-one who, once he hung up, indicated was going to call Brussels and Washington, DC.

During our conversation, a nurse came in to advise us that Agent Brown's condition had not changed, but he had been admitted and was being moved to a room in the intensive care unit on the seventh floor. The room was 717, and I would be able to go visit in about fifteen minutes.

It was getting late, 7:00 p.m., but I wanted to go see Agent Brown before I went to my hotel. Jim Dryer offered to drive me to the hotel I was staying at in Stockholm, and I gladly accepted his offer.

Jim Dryer waited while I went upstairs to check on Agent Brown. When I walked into Room 717, he was lying in a bed in the center of the room, with multiple machines hooked up to him, some making hissing sounds as they pumped life into him and others, masses of tubes and clear lines feeding liquids into his still body.

I walked up beside him and said hello and that I hoped he would be better soon, and that I would be back in the morning to see him. I patted Agent Brown on the shoulder and said good night.

As I took the elevator back downstairs I felt the weight of the world on me, but I knew I was more than capable of getting him back home. As my Grandmother Irene always used to say, "Just cool it, and do one thing at a time, and it will be all right, Maggie."

When I walked back into the waiting room, Jim Dryer asked how Agent Brown looked. I said, "Not real good; he has a lot of machinery hooked up to him, but let's see what tomorrow brings."

I stopped at the nurses' station and said good night, thanked them, and said I would see them tomorrow. I inquired about visiting hours and the nurse said that I could come anytime. Again, I thanked her and Jim Dryer, and headed for the parking garage.

The drive to the hotel took over an hour. During the drive, Jim, per his request that I call him by his first name, told me a little about the city of Stockholm, I think to pass the time, and to perhaps to distract me.

Jim said that Stockholm is located on Sweden's south-central east coast, where Lake Malaren meets the Baltic Sea. The central parts of the city consist of fourteen islands that are continuous with the Stockholm archipelago. The center of the city is situated on water; over thirty percent of the city area is made up of waterways, and another thirty percent is made up of parks and green space. I could see that this was a beautiful and lovely city. Jim told me he had been stationed here for four years, and had just signed up for another four-year tour of duty. He met his wife here, had two children and another one of the way. Jim expressed the desire never to leave, but he knew after this tour he would be going back stateside for a few years. That was a standard requirement for State Department employees so they wouldn't forget their loyalties to the United States.

By the time Jim dropped me off at the hotel, it was close to 10:00 p.m. He parked the car in front of the hotel, got Agent Brown's and my bags out of the trunk, and walked into the hotel with me. After I was checked in, he gave me his business card and said to call him any time day or night if I needed anything or if anything changed with Agent Brown. He said he would be calling me in the morning as well. I thanked him, and the bellman assisted me with my bags up to my room.

It was still daylight and everything felt surreal to me. I was hungry, tired, and wired all at the same time. I went into the bathroom, turned on the cold water, cupped my hands, filling them with cold water, and splashed water on my face several times, before grabbing a hand towel and patting my face dry. *It's going to be all right, Maggie; somehow it's going to be okay*, I thought as I walked out of the bathroom.

I went back downstairs in search of food and was directed to a restaurant directly next door to the hotel. The hotel I was staying in was small and cozy, but did not have a restaurant. I walked outside to find it warm and pleasant, for it was May here, and summer was soon to arrive with temperatures in the high sixties to low seventies. *Ahhh, it feels so good to be outside*, I thought, and it was still daylight, which was something I had never experienced before at 10:30 p.m. Due to the city's high northerly latitude, daylight varies from more than eighteen hours around midsummer, to only around six hours in late December. I was glad that I was here when it was sunny versus dark, because my mood was already dark enough from the events of the morning.

After dinner, I walked back to the hotel, nodding to the front desk clerk as I walked toward the elevator to my room. I could feel the fatigue wrapping itself around me like a warm blanket, and I knew it was time to try to get some sleep. I had no idea what tomorrow would bring, but I knew it would be another long day.

My hotel room was small but stylish, with modern furniture, the bed sitting on a platform close to the floor. The quilt on the bed was thick and inviting. I used the blackout curtains to block out the sunlight, crawled into bed, and fell into a fast and deep sleep. I dreamed about Agent Brown, his home, his family, and his frustration about being on this trip in the first place, and considering what had happened.

I woke up early, knowing that I needed a cup of coffee and a run. I pulled back the curtains to find a beautiful sunny day. I looked out the window and saw water and parks everywhere, and decided to go for a run and find coffee when I returned.

I quickly got up, got dressed in my running shorts, long-sleeved shirt, and my trusty running shoes. I stopped at the front desk and got directions to Djurgarder Park, which was in the center of town and just a few blocks from the hotel. The desk clerk assured me that I couldn't get lost, but gave me the number to the hotel just in case!

When I stepped outside, it was cooler than the night before, but I already knew that it exactly the right temperature for a run in the park. And run I did. Djurgarden Park was gorgeous, with paths leading to small bridges that carried me across waterways full of ducks and various birds. The grass, plants, and trees were all in bloom, rising from their winter slumber to greet me at every turn and step that my feet took. It was the perfect antidote to the sadness that awaited me in Room 717 at the Karolinska Hospital.

I ran for nearly an hour. I ran in one direction for a half hour, turned around, and ran back along the same route so I wouldn't get lost. When I got back to the hotel I was tired, but mentally prepared to face the day. I walked into the lobby and the front desk clerk smiled and said that I had two messages waiting for me. She handed me two pieces of paper; one with Jim Dryer's telephone number on it and the other from someone I didn't know, but it was from the hospital. I quickly asked the front desk clerk where I could get a cup of coffee and how to dial local telephone numbers.

Fortunately, there was coffee in the hotel lobby for the guests. I took two cups of coffee with sugar and milk added, and went upstairs to my room to call Jim Dryer and the hospital.

Back in my room, as I sipped my first cup of coffee, I called the hospital and spoke to the nurse at the nurses' station just outside of Agent Brown's room. The nurse advised me that they wanted to call me to let me know that there had been no change in Agent Browns condition. I thanked her and said I would be coming out later to visit him. Next, I called Jim Dryer and he asked me what the status of Agent Brown was and how I was doing. I let him know that Agent Brown's condition was the same and that I was planning on going to the hospital in a little while and would call him later that day.

I finished my coffee, showered, changed into my business attire, and went back downstairs and took a cab back to the hospital. During the ride to the hospital, I updated my trip notes, and collected my thoughts.

When I arrived back at the hospital and checked in at the nurses' station, I discovered that nothing had changed since the night before, except that Agent Brown was on life support, and his condition was stable but critical. As I made the short walk to Agent Brown's room, I was saddened both by the news, which confirmed what I had already suspected, and the feeling of melancholy for him and his family.

I scooted the chair from the corner of the room directly beside Agent Brown's bed, so I was sitting near his left forearm. I gently took his hand and said, "Good morning. I'm back and I'm going to sit with you for a while." His hand was cool, lifeless, his aged fingers showing no signs of movement as they lay against my palm. I proceed to ramble on about the hotel, the weather, my morning run, my delicious coffee, and how I thought I might go out to the airport later and find the station managers for the airlines that we were supposed to meet. I didn't think anyone had told them what had happened, and supposed they were wondering why we hadn't shown up yet today. I spent almost an hour talking about nothing, but it meant everything to me, for I had to fill the void that hung in the air with noise, a voice, life, for I knew Agent Brown's was drifting away.

Once again I stopped at the nurses' station and asked to use the telephone. I called Jim Dryer and left him a message, basically saying that there weren't any changes in Agent Brown's condition and I was heading out to the airport to work for a few hours. I let the nurse know that I would be back later that day.

Fortunately, there was a cab downstairs available to drive me out to the airport. I had the name of the station manager for American Airlines at the cargo facility, and had the cab driver drop me on the cargo side of the airport.

After paying the fare, I got out, took a deep breath, and headed for the front doors of American Airlines. Once inside, I showed the clerk my special agent credentials, along with handing him my business card, and asked to speak with Mary Torg, the station manager.

Within minutes a lovely-looking lady came from an office located somewhere behind the cargo counter, extended her hand, and greeted me warmly, welcoming me to Stockholm and saying that she had been expecting someone from the FAA. She invited me back to her office, offering me coffee or water. I gladly accepted the water as she looked at me, providing an opening to begin our conversation.

What I told her during the next few minutes, was without a doubt, not what she expected to hear. I told her what had happened to Agent Brown, why he wasn't there and why I was late. I watched her facial expression turn from that of a semi-aloof professional to a caring and concerned person. She immediately offered her assistance with anything I might need.

The only thing I could think of was having her help me notify the other three station managers we were supposed to see this week, and advise them of what had happened. I told her I wasn't sure yet about how much work I could get done, but I was going to try to look at some of the required security measures. I admitted that I was a bit distracted, pretty new to being overseas, but I wanted to help. Mary Torg said she would call the other managers for me and perhaps we could all get together tomorrow and see if we could collectively come up with a plan to schedule record reviews, and anything else I needed. We talked for over an hour about the airline, her job, and where they flew. Some of this information I had already learned during the briefings back in Brussels, but it was always good to hear information more than once, and direct from the airline. We planned to meet again tomorrow morning at 11:00. Mary Torg called a cab for me and I went back to the hospital to check on Agent Brown.

I ended up staying at the hospital until 6:00 p.m. when one of the nurses finally shooed me out, saying, "Dear one, nothing more can be done. He's in God's hands now. I want you to go get some dinner and some rest."

Reluctantly, I knew she was right, so I reached over and patted Agent Brown gently on the top of his head, saying, "Good night. I'll see you tomorrow." I headed downstairs into the bright and sunny evening, which felt more gloomy and dark to me.

When I got back to the hotel, I decided to go for another run, following the same route as I had earlier that day. My mood was so dark that I wanted to run until I couldn't breathe. *I feel so damn alone*, I thought. But I knew I had to keep going.

After my run, I changed, went next door to the restaurant and ate, alone and in silence. I was tired, but I knew sleep was not going to come easy.

The next morning I repeated my steps almost exactly from the time I got out of bed, up until my meeting at 11:00 at the airport. I had gone to see Agent Brown and confirmed that his condition remained unchanged. I called Jim Dryer, who notified me that he had been in contact with the embassy in Brussels and that one of the agents from the FAA by the name of Dick Scripps was flying to Stockholm tomorrow to assist me. *Assistance*, I thought to myself, *I wonder what that will entail?*

When I arrived at the meeting at the American Airlines office at the airport, Mary Torg greeted me warmly, quietly asking, "How was your evening?" I briefly updated her that Agent Brown's condition was the same and that another agent from the FAA, Dick Scripps, was flying in tomorrow to assist. "I assume he's going to assist me with conducting the assessments here, but I'm not one hundred percent sure of that. I'll let you know," I said.

The meeting with Mary and the other two station managers was cordial, organized, and productive. They listened intently as I described the events of the last two days and, like Mary, offered any assistance in any way that they could. It was really heartwarming for them to be so concerned about complete strangers.

The schedule we created allowed me to visit Agent Brown at the hospital in the morning and begin our assessment schedule at 11:00 a.m. Thursday and Friday of that week, and Monday through Friday of the next week. The plan was fluid, due to the situation at hand, but a plan that can be modified is better than no plan at all. Mary handed me off to one of her cargo agents and for the next few hours I began looking at cargo records. I left later that day with confidence that things were getting done, and headed back to the hospital.

"I know, I know, I'm leaving," I said to the same nurse who shooed me out a few days ago, once again near 7:00 p.m. today. Yet, somehow I felt compelled to stay; Agent Brown didn't have anyone here, and I felt responsible — or in charge might be more accurate; in charge that somehow it would be incumbent upon me to get him home. Jim Dryer had let me know earlier in the day that Agent Brown's wife would not be flying over due to health reasons, and the embassy was trying to decide if they were going to arrange for a medical flight back to the United States. The cost would be enormous, so the red tape was even more substantial than normal, he said with a grim tone in his voice.

Back at the hotel, I changed, ran, ate, and went to bed. I was exhausted, but determined to get two jobs done: one, to do what I could for Agent Brown; and two, to get some work done so I'd make good on my paycheck, as my dad always said.

Thursday morning was another picture-perfect day for a run. Today I ran at 6:00 a.m., farther and farther along the paths in the park, over bridges, around water, taking in all of the beauty of this beautiful city, feeling downcast, in shock, but very alert, as if my mind were in full emergency response mode, always on the alert. When I got back to the hotel, I grabbed my lukewarm coffee, quickly changed, and headed back to the hospital.

Agent Brown was quietly waiting for me, fast asleep in world of void. "Hello, my friend," I said as I began talking about the events of day after I left yesterday, and how my run went that morning. I just wanted to talk; it wasn't at all important, it was just my voice in a quiet room, except for the breathing machine that was now keeping Agent Brown alive. He was attached to other life-sustaining equipment as well — the names I didn't know, nor did I ever want to know.

When I arrived at the American Airlines office at the airport a few hours later, I found Mary there speaking with someone I didn't know. Her facial expression carried a deep frown and a slowly growing hint of disgust. I didn't know Mary well, but over the past few days, I had gotten to know her as a fair person, a very knowledgeable person, caring and skilled both professionally and personally. So I wondered why she didn't appear to like this individual. Unfortunately, I found out the answer, sadly, only too quickly. The man who stood before us was none other than Agent Dick Scripps. Our introduction was uncomfortable; he hugged me as if he knew me, and I immediately pulled back, wanting to punch him in the face. *What a jerk!* I thought. I could see that Mary was thinking the exact same thing.

Needless to say, over the next few hours everything that Mary, the three other station managers, and I had scheduled and agreed on was undone by my fellow colleague. I was embarrassed, but unable to stop him because he was stationed in Brussels and his office had direct oversight for this part of the world. I was a guest.

Once the meeting was over, Agent Scripps suggested we all meet again first thing tomorrow morning, and asked Mary to call a taxi for him so he could go to the hotel. I, on the other hand, was going back to the hospital to check on Agent Brown and I would find my own taxi. Before I left, I asked Mary if I could make a copy of my assessment notes that I had taken yesterday, because I wanted to give a copy to Agent Scripps so there was no duplication of work. She showed me where the copier was. I quickly made my copies, and said I would come out tomorrow to see what I could do to assist. She smiled; no words were spoken as I headed back to find Agent Scripps so I could give him a copy of what I had already completed.

And once again I was off, taking a cab back to the hospital, only this time I was leaving Mary Torg with Agent Scripps and his ego.

Thursday passed; I slept fitfully, awaking at 0430 to the ringing telephone in my hotel room. It was a nurse from the hospital informing me that Agent Brown's condition continued unchanged and that the physician on duty last night had recommended that Agent Brown be taken off life support.

I sat up with a jolt, and said, "Please don't take him off life support until I get there. Please." The nurse promised, and I was dressed and just about out the door before I hung up the telephone.

I arrived at the hospital at 0600 hours and headed up the elevator to the nurses' station. The nurse on duty saw me step off the elevator and nodded as I walked toward her. She informed me that Agent Brown was still on life support and that the doctor had agreed to wait for my arrival.

When I walked into Room 717, everything appeared unchanged. Agent Brown hadn't moved in five days. He was as lifeless this morning as he had been when I first saw him in this very room Monday evening. The line indicating brain activity was flat and his heartbeat unchanging due to the mechanical beast that was assisting him. I sat down beside him, talking quietly, again about nothing, just filling the void, as I now knew that he too had a void deep inside him. I put my head down on his forearm and said, "I'm sorry, Ed, I'm so sorry," as my tears fell, dripping onto the sheet that lay beneath him.

I stood, walked around to the foot of his bed, placed my hand on his foot, and said, "It's time to go home, Ed. I'm taking you home now." With that, the brain wave monitor made one beep, and the heart monitor one last flicker, and then everything flat lined again. I knew he had heard me; he knew I was taking him back to his beloved wife, family, and home.

The nurse came into the room in response to the equipment alarms, as I then silently left the room, knowing she still had a job to do. I went back into the waiting room, sat down, collected my thoughts, walked back to the nurses' station, and asked to use the telephone so I could call Jim Dryer.

When that strong Southern accent answered the phone at 0630, I knew that I had just awakened him, but this was a necessary call. I imagined that he too, as I had a few hours earlier, sat straight up in bed when I relayed the events that had just taken place.

As I held back my tears I said, "He passed, Jim; Agent Brown was just taken off life support."

"I'm on my way," Jim said. "I'll see you within the hour."

It would take three days to arrange for transport to get Agent Brown home. Friday was spent talking with Jim Dryer as he relayed information back between the Embassy in Brussels and Washington, DC. I kept my journal, and kept my wits about me. I now knew that Agent Scripps was staying in the same hotel, but our paths thankfully barely crossed.

Agent Scripps was originally from Atlanta, Georgia, and seemed to have that old-fashioned idea that women were creatures who were completely helpless. I'm not sure how he'd survived this long in government service, but somehow he managed to stay beneath the radar, for I found him to be a complete chauvinist, an idiot, and basically a jerk. I had been in the country for a week, handling a serious medical crisis, along with doing the assignment that I was sent originally to do. When Agent Brown passed away, I guess I was supposed to crumble. God knows I was sad, exhausted, and ready to go home, but I had promised myself I would get Agent Brown home, and that's exactly what I was going to do. So when Agent Dick Scripps tired to treat me as a defenseless lady, I got a little testy. "Mad Dog" came to the surface with a vengeance. I was professional and polite, but I had no desire to go sightseeing or share a meal with Agent Scripps. Agents Scripps wasn't a runner, so we went our separate ways over the weekend.

I ran, walked, and ran more, for two days. Eat, sleep, and run, that's all I did. I don't know how many miles I logged, but it was more than I had ever run in my life.

I let the sun, the fresh air, and the beauty of the lakes, parks, and people fill my thoughts with optimism and strength. "Get through the weekend, Maggie. You've got to get Ed home now," I said as I ran mile after mile. The weekend passed, Monday morning came, and the first call I made was to Jim Dryer to see if there were any news. And there was.

Authorization had been made to fly Agent Brown home on Wednesday on Swiss Air from Stockholm to John F. Kennedy (JFK) Airport. I was to escort his body home and then fly on to Washington, DC for a debriefing. Jim asked if I could come out to the embassy later that day, after lunch, around 2:00 p.m., and he would give me my tickets for JFK. I said that would be perfect and I went downstairs to meet Agent Scripps so we could head out to the airport to work.

I met Agent Scripps in the lobby at 0900 hours, found a taxi, and we headed for the airport. We talked about Agent Brown for a few minutes, but mainly we talked about airport assessments and how things were going at the airport. Everything seemed to be fine, and Agent Scripps thought he might be able to travel on either Thursday or Friday back to Brussels. I was glad for him; even if I thought he was a bit of a jerk, he had stepped into a situation without warning or notice and tried to make order of it. I still didn't like the fact that he changed a perfectly good game plan, but some people just had to change things around to feel in control. It didn't take me long to realize that Agent Scripps was one of those types of people — a control freak. Sadly, the people who suffered at the hands of control freaks like Agent Scripps were the people we kept changing our minds on. In this case it was the airline station managers.

Jim Dryer was in his office when I arrived promptly at 2:00 that afternoon. When he saw me enter, he stood up and walked from behind his desk and shook my hand. "Are you all right? Do you need anything?" he said.

"No, I'm fine; at this point I just need to get Agent Brown home, and then myself home. It's time to go home, Jim," I said quietly. Jim picked up a packet from his desk and proceeded to give me all of my flight information in New York. We talked for about an hour before we said our goodbyes. I couldn't thank him enough for facilitating all of the telephone calls between Brussels and Washington, DC, and a couple of very difficult telephone calls to Agent Brown's wife back in Baltimore.

On Tuesday morning, I saw Agent Scripps in the hotel lobby as he was getting ready to leave for the airport. He told me that everything was fine at the airport, so he had scheduled a flight for Wednesday afternoon for Brussels. I let him know that I was going to the hospital this morning to sign all the documentation releasing Agent Brown into my custody, and then heading out to the airport to make sure the flight arrangements were complete and that Agent Brown and I would be traveling on the same aircraft back to New York. We shook hands, and said our goodbyes, since we would not be seeing each other again this trip. We left the hotel together, each catching a taxi, his for a ride to the airport, and mine to the Karolinska for one last visit.

At the hospital, I went to the business office and signed all the necessary paperwork releasing Agent Brown to my guardianship. I had never traveled with this type of responsibility, so I did my usual note-taking, winging it with common sense, a somber smile, and professional attitude. I took the elevator upstairs one last time, hoping to see a few of the nurses who had been so gracious to me. As I stepped off the elevator, the two nurses at the nurses' station looked up, recognized me, and smiled. I walked over and thanked them for being so kind, and we hugged one another. A few minutes later as I rode the elevator back downstairs, I knew I would never forget the kindness of strangers, and the professional care the doctors, nurses, and staff of this fine hospital had afforded Agent Brown. I wished the outcome had been better, but it was not meant to be.

At the airport, I went to the cargo facility office for Swiss Air, identified myself, and asked if there were anything further that I needed to do to facilitate getting Agent Brown back stateside. The agent checked on his computer, looked at various pieces of paperwork — both what he had on file and what I presented— and said everything appeared to be in order. I thanked him and headed back out to find a taxi for the last ride back to the hotel.

Thankfully, government employees are given federal credit cards when they travel on official business, because the amount of money that I had spent to date on taxi rides was enormous. Each ride between the airport, the hotel, or the hospital cost about $45 US dollars each way. I figured I was spending about $150 a day on taxi rides.

I took one last two-hour run before it was time to pack, sleep, and head back to the airport in the morning. My twelve-hour flight to JFK was scheduled to leave at 10:00 a.m. and I needed to be at the airport three hours prior to departure. I knew it was going to be another sleepless night, but at least the US Embassy here had booked me in business class for the ride home. It's a luxury not normally afforded to government employees but someone, somewhere, authorized the upgrade, one I was willing to accept.

Sleep avoided me like a cat avoids being given a bath. I think I would have felt better if I had just stayed up all night. I kicked, I tossed, and I dreamed about Agent Brown, his family, airport and air carrier assessments, air marshal training, old boyfriends, the possibility of future boyfriends; you name it, I dreamt it. I must have looked like hell when I finally gave up at 3:00 a.m. and got up. I took a long hot steamy shower, got dressed, finished packing, and paced around the tiny room for another thirty minutes before I went downstairs with my bag dragging behind me, looking for a cup of coffee.

I piled myself into a taxi at 0530, waved goodbye to this lovely city, and headed for the airport, the daylight still shining.

The ticket counter line to check in for the flight was thicker and longer than I thought it would be so early in the morning. Obviously other people were just as anxious to get home as I was. My turn finally came and I proceeded to the counter, presented my ticket and passport, and placed Agent Brown's and my checked luggage beside me. The agent asked me to place my bags on the scale to be weighed. She soon discovered, as I did, that I had exceeded the baggage allowance for one traveler, the consequences being an additional baggage charge of $250. I had to ask the agent twice, as I couldn't believe my ears that I was being charged for excess baggage. I briefly explained that the owner of one suitcase had passed away, and I was escorting his remains back to his family. The explanation fell on deaf ears. Eventually I paid the additional $250, or Agent Brown's bag would not have been allowed onboard.

I walked away, slightly peeved, but fully awake now, and completely ready to go home. The Swiss Air Agent was only doing her job, but sometimes doing your job can be really poor customer service. As I was walking toward the checkpoint, Mary Torg called out my name. I was so surprised to see her on this side of the airport, and we greeted one another as long-lost friends. Mary told me that she had wanted to give me a small gift as a token of appreciation and friendship, and for being so professional under such difficult circumstances. She gave me a small package containing four small ivory-colored handkerchiefs, each with one hand-embroidered butterfly, surrounded by delicate lace. What a gesture of kindness from someone who had been a stranger less than two weeks ago. She asked how my morning was, and if I needed anything prior to boarding. When I offhandedly told her about paying for Agent Brown's bag, not thinking too much about it, she became furious and started walking me back to the ticket counter.

Mary said, "Wait for just a minute," and she walked to the counter, and began speaking to the agent. Both Mary's and the agent's hands were moving back and forth as each explained their position regarding the checked luggage. In the end, Mary prevailed, coming back with cash in hand, full of apologies. She too was fully awake, and needed to return to work. And I needed to board an aircraft for home.

We said our goodbyes with hearty handshakes, hugs, and smiles. I turned and headed for the security checkpoint, my gate, and my duty to get Agent Brown home.

CHAPTER **Nine**

Who The Hell Are You?

WITH THE SCREENING process behind me, I walked the long terminal, watching people, watching life scurrying by, with destinations unknown, except my own. I found the Swiss Air departure gate, the flight board saying the flight was on time — fingers crossed it remained that way, for I had an hour and a half to wait.

I walked over to the window, unintentionally, but just in time to see Agent Brown's casket being loaded in the aft cargo compartment of the aircraft. I was sitting in business class this morning, so we would be almost at opposite ends of the plane. At least I had confirmation that he had been boarded, for a flight that he never imagined he'd be taking when he started this mission just a few weeks before. It was a wake-up call, a reminder to me that life is precious, full of surprises, and sometimes way too short. At that moment, more than anything I wanted to go home, wanted to be with someone, two worlds colliding, fighting off the loneliness that creeps into your life when you're not looking, but fills you with despair when you least expect it.

Soon the number of persons in the waiting area began increasing, the slight rise in noise, the shuffling of luggage stuffed to the gills, so the one carry-on item per person requirement could be met. I always wondered why travelers had to take so much stuff. What was the necessity? I carried a small backpack, which was not full, by any means, and I seemed to get along just fine.

The agent at the gate said good morning to everyone in the board-ing area in two languages: Swedish, and English. She explained the boarding process and asked that families with small children and the elderly be boarded first.

When it was my turn to board, I gave my boarding pass to the agent, said thank you, and walked down the jetway and onto the DC-10 for the long flight home.

Business class was just past first class; the cabin and the seats were arranged with two seats each on the left, middle, and right sides of the aircraft. Two by two by two is the vernacular used by the airlines to describe this 248- passenger capacity DC-10, accommodating 12 passengers in first class, 36 in business, and 200 in coach. My seat as-signment was 4D, the first row in business class, middle row. I could see almost all the way to the cockpit but not quite; a partition separat-ing the forward galley from first class blocked my full view. I liked the partition being there, because more leg room had been created for bulkhead seats. An added bonus was putting my feet on the partition to rest.

I was snuggled in my seat, beginning to feel my heart rate slow, along with a huge sense of sadness beginning to overtake me. On the one hand, I was elated to be heading home; but on the other, I was saddened that Agent Brown, even if he had been a grump to me, was not alive to travel home to his wife and family. "It will be all right, Maggie," I said to myself. "Your mission is almost complete; you're going home, and it will be all right."

Just as I finished those thoughts, a man dressed in khaki slacks, navy-blue polo shirt, and sports jacket dropped his bag in seat 4C and said hello as he smiled down at me. His grin was enormous, showing a mouthful of teeth — some crooked, some straight, but all very, very white. "Hello," he said.

"Hi," I said in return, as he proceeded to get all of his things jammed into the overhead compartment above except for a book, glasses, and one of those funny neck pillows. It was not only funny-looking; it was bright orange, with a Saab logo on it. I took it for granted that he was a businessman on travel, who worked for Saab, and was in need of some down time to read and nap. I hoped so, anyway, for I was in need of a nap myself.

The flight attendant stopped at our seats and asked if we would like anything to drink. "Water for me, please," I said, and the gentleman next to me asked for a Coke. When our drinks and a warm mixed assortment of nuts arrived, the gentleman turned and introduced himself as Ray. I told him my name and he began chatting away, asking a million questions, to ascertain if I was on holiday, business, or what. I immediately knew that he had a very inquisitive mind, and all thoughts and hopes of resting on this flight might not be an option.

With the front door closed, the emergency evacuation slides armed, and safety briefings complete, the flight attendants were all seated as the DC-10 taxied for take-off. I was ready for this bird to fly, to begin my long distance escape from one continent to another, one segment of a tragedy to another, landing at a final destination for Agent Brown and myself.

As we lifted off, I could only feel us pulling away from the ground; the windows were too far away to see, but for now, feeling the lift was enough. I felt myself releasing the breath I was so dearly holding onto inside my lungs.

Earlier versions of the DC-10 had a serious defect in their aft cargo doors; the locking pins on the doors weren't long enough to adequately secure them. Three accidents in 1972, 1974, and 1979 had occurred before McDonnell Douglas issued a warning to airlines to change the locking mechanisms on their cargo doors. *So far, so good* I thought, but I always had a twinge of controlled anticipation when flying on a DC-10, knowing the history of these aircraft, always hoping the airline I was flying on followed the sage advice of McDonnell Douglas. Some overseas carriers didn't listen; I recall one airline losing 346 lives in a 1974 crash just outside of Paris. However, I wasn't going to worry anymore; we were airborne, I was in business class, I had just reclined my seat, and I felt my eyes closing for a much-needed nap.

When I woke up, Ray was snoring loudly next to me, which made me chuckle. My neck and shoulders were stiff from sleeping in an upright position, but by the grace of God, I don't think I snored. Well, if I did, I didn't keep Ray awake!

I looked at my watch and saw that I had slept for over an hour. I unbuckled my seatbelt, stood up, looked around, and walked two rows back to the lavatory located between rows six and seven in business class.

Inside, I pulled the door shut, locked it, and looked at myself in the mirror, shaking my head slowing from side to side, thinking that I looked pretty good considering the circumstances. I washed my face and hands, and pulled my hair away from my face before leaving the lavatory. I decided to do a loop around the aircraft before I returned to my seat. I headed toward the back of the plane, walking straight down the left aisle, ending at row thirty-eight, and then moved across and walked back up the right side of the aircraft until I reached my seat. It felt good to get up. I wasn't in anyone's way, since no service carts were out yet, and most of my fellow passengers were napping like Ray was.

When I got back to my seat, Ray was still sleeping, so I stole a couple of seconds to take a look at him. His head was slumped over and I could see that most of the hair on the top of his head had disappeared. It was cut short, and he didn't bother to do that wave thing that so many men do when they have hair loss. He was getting gray, but the blond still predominated, as if in a fight for life with the gray hair to stay young. I didn't know if he was a runner, but he was pretty thin, appeared to be in pretty good shape, and wore an expensive Swiss Army watch. While he was asleep that was all I could assess, so I settled back into my seat and began reading a *Runner's World* magazine for the fifth time, I suspected. I had carried this magazine with me since I left home just a few weeks before, and when everything went south with Agent Brown, this magazine, somehow, became my link with home, vitality, and life, so I kept it even though it had been read multiple times.

Ray began stirring in the seat next to mine, jerking his head up, and then rocking it from side to side, as I had done earlier, to work out the knots from sleeping while sitting up. He unbuckled his seatbelt, got up, and walked toward the lavatory, disappearing inside, as I had done earlier as well. Seemed like an airplane ritual that never changed, no matter who the traveler was.

As soon as the flight attendants began the lunch service, the passengers came in droves to the lavatories, stretching, talking, and holding on to the seat backrests as they stood in line. Ray and I were unaffected, since the lavatories were behind us and first class had their own facilities, but I stood for a while, my back resting on the partition, watching, listening, and waiting … waiting to get home.

While lunch was served, Ray and I talked; mostly he talked about his job, the advertising world, his wife, kids, and tennis. It turned out that Ray and his wife played tennis, mostly doubles, and they were pretty good, according to their tennis club standings. His world was so different from mine; it was really interesting to hear about his life.

"So what do you do for a living?" Ray asked.

"I work for the government, for the Federal Aviation Administration. Been with the FAA for almost two years now, and, as you are, I'm returning home from a business trip," I said. I immediately realized I was almost holding my breath, in case he decided to probe more about my trip. Fortunately, he didn't probe, and we began talking about the hassles of checkpoint screening, hearing his nightmare experiences, as every frequent traveler insists on telling anyone that will listen. I didn't say much, just listened, for I understood that most people didn't really care to be screened, but they understood that it was a necessary evil of traveling.

We passed a great deal of the flight by talking, watching movies, and napping. I couldn't escape the down time, but I was antsy, ready to get to New York, and meet the agents who were meeting my flight.

About three hours before we landed, the captain announced over the loud speaker that we would be landing at JFK Airport one and an half hours ahead of schedule due to a Government VIP onboard, and that air traffic control had given this flight special air space jurisdiction to make a direct flight path to New York. The captain advised the flight attendants to expedite their food service, and for the passengers to be prepared to deplane a little ahead of schedule today. Everyone in the cabin clapped when the captain finished his announcement.

Ray agreed, along with everyone else, that earlier was better, and said out loud, "I wonder who the VIP is, and the reason for the early landing." I didn't answer; I sat quietly, for I had a strong suspicion that Agent Brown might be the VIP onboard.

The Swiss Air flight did land, as the captain predicted, at JFK Airport almost two hours ahead of schedule. The early arrival didn't help those passengers who had connections, like Ray did, but at least they were on the ground, didn't have to worry about tight connections, and could walk around more freely.

The DC-10 pulled up to the gate; flight attendants advised the passengers that it was all right to unbuckle their seatbelts, and the two left forward doors on the aircraft opened.

A gentleman walked onboard; taking a microphone, he welcomed everyone to JFK and indicated where the baggage claim area was located. He also asked that everyone remain seated. Federal Aviation Administration Special Agents were boarding to escort one passenger off the aircraft first.

Two agents rapidly appeared onboard, and walked into the first class section, and then directly over to my seat. They greeted me by saying, "Welcome to JFK, Agent Stewart; please come with us."

Ray, momentarily stunned, turned, looked at me, and said, "Who the hell are you?"

As I picked up my bag, slightly stunned myself, I turned and said, "I'm just trying to get someone home. It was nice chatting with you, Ray. Bye."

I got off the aircraft with one agent in front of me, and one behind me.

The captain was standing at the cockpit door as I left the aircraft. He thanked me for my service, for a job well done, and the fastest flight from Sweden to JFK that he had ever flown!

For the second time, in a matter of minutes, now I was stunned.

Talk about feeling like a celebrity, although a reluctant one. It was mayhem beyond the jet bridge door. There were at least four other agents milling about, quickly standing not at attention, but certainly in straighter postures than they'd had seconds before when they saw us walking out the jetway bridge. We stood in a circle: the agent in charge, Reggie Masters, introduced himself, and briefly introduced everyone else in the group. Agent Masters informed me that my luggage was being unloaded, priority handling for US Customs clearance would take place, and we were going to a conference room at the American Airlines Terminal, where I would be meeting with Agent Brown's wife and two of his sons.

As Agent Masters began directing me toward the American Airlines terminal, I asked him what was going on with Agent Brown's casket. Agent Masters said that it was being transferred from this flight to another carrier for the short trip to Baltimore International Airport (BWI). "Agent Masters, I want to go ramp side before we go over to American Airlines so I can say goodbye to Agent Brown," I said, my voice sounding firmer than it needed to be.

Agent Masters furrowed his brow, but turned to one of the other agents and said, "Get us ramp side ASAP."

I walked down the metal stairs, actually aware of each footstep, knowing in my heart that my mission was almost complete. The casket sat beneath the undercarriage of the DC-10, alone, the afternoon sun barely shining on this May Day. It was as if the sky had turned gloomy, in honor and recognition of the fallen special agent who lay inside the black wooden casket.

I walked over, placed my hand on his casket, and said, "Okay, my friend, you're home. Now your family will be able to get you to your place of rest. I am truly sorry, Agent Brown." As I turned and walked away, toward the stairs leading back to the mini chaos inside the terminal, I felt a sadness that the last leg of this journey for Agent Brown would be alone, realizing that I too was alone.

Chaos was a slight understatement. Agent Masters had everyone from his office out at the airport doing something, necessary or not. I truly did appreciate the accelerated flight times, clearing customs with virtually no questions asked, and then being allowed to say farewell to Agent Brown — as for the rest, it was overwhelming.

Now came the difficult part: meeting Agent Brown's wife, Claire, and two sons. When I entered the American Airlines conference room, seated at the table was an older woman, tired, deep bags surrounding her eyes, her gray hair slightly disheveled, handkerchief in hand; it was clear she had been crying. By the looks of her, I don't think she had stopped crying since being given the terrible news of her husband's death. Her sons were stooped beside her, one leaning over her chair, the other kneeling beside her, consoling her as best they could, looking as if they needed consoling too.

The sons stood when our entourage entered the room, assisting their mother to her feet, and ambling over toward us. I walked slightly ahead of Agent Masters and took Mrs. Brown's hand and told her, "Hello, Mrs. Brown; I'm Maggie Stewart."

The floodgates really opened and she cried, hugged me, and continued to cry, with an occasional sob, followed by a million questions. "What happened? Did he suffer? Did he know where he was? Could you talk to him? Where were you when he got sick?" I led her back to a chair, where she half-crumpled, half-sat down, as I pulled a chair out, turning it sideways to face her, held her hands, and began answering all of her questions.

The biggest relief I could give her was letting her know how much he really wanted to be home with her, mowing the grass, tending to his pool, enjoying barbeques with his family, before the brief summer turned to fall and winter once again. I told Claire that he had told me all of this while we were in Brussels, waiting to travel to Stockholm. He loved his family dearly, and he really wanted to be home, but he understood duty, too.

Our conversation, which lasted twenty minutes, was filled with tears, sadness, and a numb sense that reality was taking place for this family, before my very eyes, that their beloved husband, father, and friend was gone forever. The aneurysm that took Agent Brown's life had taken a part of theirs too. I think one of the hardest parts for everyone, besides his death, was that no one got to say goodbye.

The Browns were Catholic, and I would be lighting several candles for them once I got home. But for now, I could only give them all one last hug, since it was time for me fly to Washington, DC and debrief the events of the past two weeks.

Agent Masters dismissed the rest of the team and walked me to my gate. I thanked him for everything that he had done. He handed me my airline tickets for Washington National Airport, and gave me the name of the hotel I would be staying at; we shook hands, and he wished me well.

When I landed at Washington National Airport (DCA), thankfully, no one was there to meet me. I was staying at the Holiday Inn on SW 9th Street, which I was told was directly across the street from FAA Headquarters, so I could walk to the office the next morning.

I took a cab from the airport to the hotel and was able to see the Washington Monument, Jefferson Memorial, and the Smithsonian. I had never been to Washington, DC so I was already spellbound by the few historical landmarks I had seen only on television until now.

I pushed the revolving door leading into the Holiday Inn, feeling the weight of the world on my shoulders. I dragged my bag behind me, feeling its weight, hearing the tiny suitcase wheels clacking along on the flooring behind me. "Progress," I said to myself. "Just keep moving forward."

It was getting late, and as I walked toward the front desk, I could see that it was empty. I checked in for my two-night stay, asked and was told that the restaurant would be open until 11:00 p.m., so I had about an hour to get something to eat.

I found my way to my room, dropped my bag, went back downstairs, and found the first available seat at the bar to get a drink and some dinner. The bartender greeted me with a big smile. "May I have a glass of white wine, please?"

"Absolutely, dear," he purred while pouring me a glass, just about brimful. He said with a smile, "Sort of looks like you're in need of a glass of wine."

"If you only knew," I said as I tipped my glass to him and took my first sip, which was divine. I looked the menu over, and ordered a Caesar salad and garlic toast. When my food came I ordered another glass of wine and sat back to enjoy the most delicious salad I had ever eaten.

I didn't set an alarm, since I didn't know what time anyone expected me the next morning. I indulged, leaving Mother Nature to wake me up. At 0430 I was wide awake! My room had a coffee maker, so I made myself a cup of coffee, looked out the window at the darkened street below, and decided to stretch, get dressed, and go for a run. I figured by the time I got myself organized, and had coffee, daylight would be just peeking up near the dome of the Capitol building directly to the east of me.

The night before, the bartender had told me that when I left the hotel, I could walk two blocks to the office in a westerly direction, and one block to the north of my office, where I would find "The Mall." The Mall was the strip of ground, some grass, and some sand-paved walk, surrounded by the Capitol, the Washington Monument, the Smithsonian, and multiple other museums along a mile-long route. It was easy to find, easy to run on the dirt path, and there wouldn't be any lack of company, for many of the young, eager Washingtonians would be out for an early-morning run before their pressure-filled and politically driven careers took over for the day.

At 0545 I was out the door, heading west as directed, and easily found the L'Enfant Plaza Metro Station, the Federal Aviation Headquarters Building on 7th S.W. and Independence, and The Mall one block ahead to the north.

As soon as I set foot on the dirt path, I felt a rise of patriotism I had never felt before. My emotions were strong as I ran past the Smithsonian, with the Washington Monument looming in front of me, a giant pillar rising from the ground, commanding attention. As I ran, runners were passing me with lightning speed, all fully concentrating on the task at hand, barely looking around, much less at the rich history that surrounded them. I turned the corner, headed past the Washington Monument and turned toward the Capitol. I ran past the Museum of American History, the Natural History Museum, the National Gallery, the reflection pool, and up the Capitol steps. Wow! I was so energized that I felt as if I could run forever, but I knew I had to turn again, and run back toward the hotel. It was full daylight by the time I passed the Botanic Garden and the Air and Space Museum. I vowed to visit all of these places someday, and then turned down 9th Street to find my hotel.

By the time I had cleaned up, had breakfast, and walked over to the Federal Aviation Building, it was 0830 in the morning. I didn't even know what floor I had to go to, so after presenting my identification at the door, I asked which floor the security office was on, and was directed to the elevator bank and told to go to the third floor.

When I stepped off the elevator, I still didn't know where I was supposed to go. The hallway was very generic in color and design. All of the doorways looked identical; the floor tiling was a shiny gray military-style color, and exactly the same. People were scurrying up and down the halls, without a care in the world that a stranger was amongst them; they were all climbing to the top, with important things to do, and places to go. Me, I just wanted to go home. But I went eenie, meenie, minie, moe, and picked a direction and headed to the biggest doorway I could see. Amazingly, I had guessed correctly, for as I approached the double doors, I could read the painted words: "Office of Aviation Security" (ACS) printed in square gold letters on the glass.

"Here we go. Maggie Stewart is in the building," I said to myself as I pulled back my shoulders and walked through those double glass doors.

The next few minutes were a bit confusing, because no one was exactly sure whom I was supposed to be meeting with. Certainly, the front office staff had not been informed, I wasn't on anyone's calendar, and the two ladies sitting behind the enormous secretarial desks clearly did not know what to do with me.

Suddenly, Director Sword, hearing the inquiries, came out of his office, greeting me as if I were a long-lost relative. He asked one of the office assistants to call Special Agent Quinn to his office ASAP.

Agent Quinn must have double-timed it to the Director's Office, adhering to the old adage that when the boss calls, you'd best get there quickly.

Director Sword advised Quinn and me that today and tomorrow a few staffers were going to discuss the events, processes, and procedures that I followed when Agent Brown took ill and sadly passed away, because in the history of this organization, no one had ever experienced what had just happened. I had handled the situation with such superb professionalism that headquarters wanted to capture the process while it was fresh, so if this situation ever arose again, others wouldn't have to invent the process to follow all over again.

Director Sword shook my hand, and said again, "I am was very proud of you, Maggie, and remember that if you ever want to come to Washington, DC and work, a job is here waiting for you. You just name it!"

"Thank you ,sir," I said. "It wasn't the outcome I expected when I first went on this assessment, but I was proud to have been able to get Agent Brown home to his family." Director Sword shook my hand again, and I then followed Agent Quinn down the hall to his office.

Agent Quinn was the Deputy to the Director of Operations. On the ACS Organizational Chart this is the organizational unit within ACS that directs field operations. Eventually, if you looked down the chain far enough, you would find the LAX CASFO at the very bottom of the organizational chart. Maggie Stewart was talking to the second in command for the branch responsible for my having a job!

Agent Quinn called in two other people for this meeting, one from policy, and a second agent from emergency management. Everyone wanted to hear what happened, how I figured out what to do, and then how I had captured all of the information I was providing them on the trip report that I had written while I was in Stockholm.

"Common sense, for the most part, is the first thing I did," I said. "I was alone, I knew I needed help, I was in a foreign country, so to me, it was logical that I contact the US Embassy for assistance." Everyone nodded their heads in agreement, and I waited for the next question.

And so it went, question after question, answer after answer — everything had logic to me, a sequence of events; each event needed an action, and my reaction was to react, solving the problem one step at a time. Everyone seemed so amazed. *Why?* I thought to myself.

By the end of the day, Agent Quinn had his feet up on his desk, and with hands folded behind his head, kept asking me if I wanted to move to Washington, DC. "You name it, and we'll find you a job," Agent Quinn had said several times. I thanked him, saying that I was new to the agency, and the cadre, and wanted to continue with air marshal and special agent programs for a few more years before making any major moves to Washington. I wanted time to learn my job as a field agent. With those final words, and hearty thank yous, given by all, I was able again to call it a day.

It turned out I didn't need to stay the second day, so when I returned to my room I called American Airlines and booked a direct flight from Dulles International Airport (IAD) to Los Angeles on the red eye that was departing at 2200 hours. I headed out the door for one last run among the spectacular monuments and memorials dotted along The Mall. It was a glorious run, filled with sightseeing, dodging tourists, and running as fast as I could in an attempt to burn off the energy that was pent up inside me like a wildcat, caged and anxious to run free again at any cost.

Back at the hotel, I stopped at the front desk, explained that my business trip had ended early, and that I was flying home later that evening. The desk clerk instinctively knew that I dearly wanted to go home, and graciously honored my change of itinerary with a late check-out, charging me for only half a day versus a full one night's stay. The clerk wished me farewell, and hoped I would choose Holiday

Inn for my next business trip in Washington, DC.

Riding for an hour to Dulles Airport gave me plenty of time to reflect on the past few weeks. What a whirlwind of events: foreign travel, a death of a fellow agent, expedited air traffic control service, meeting after meeting with the highest officials in our agency, a job offer … and all I wanted was to return to the Los Angeles Field Office. It all seemed logical to me. It wasn't time for me to advance yet, and I was living close to my family again, and in California where there was so much to do, see, and enjoy. Yes, I had made the right decision; it was time to go home.

The red eye was just that — it was exhausting to fly so late, after such a meeting-packed day, and stressful few weeks. But landing at 6:00 a.m., knowing that I was finally home, somehow made it worthwhile. I was elated to see Agent Stanton standing in the boarding gate area when I deplaned.

"Hi — how did you know I was on this flight?" I said as I walked up to him.

"Oh, we have our ways," Agent Stanton said with a great big grin. "Are you up for a cup of coffee before you head home for some well-deserved sleep?"

"I sure am, especially with you. I am so glad to be home," I said as we headed toward the Starbucks in the American Airlines terminal.

We stood in line for a few minutes and chatted about what was going on in the office, and how everyone was. Everyone was fine — no new personnel, although he'd heard a rumor that the office was supposed to get a few more agents before the end of the fiscal year, which was October. He sure hoped so, because the workload was getting heavier, more travel for training, foreign airport assessments and federal air marshal trips. And management said that the work plan numbers could not be changed per Washington, DC, so somehow, some way, the work would have to get done. At least overtime had been authorized, which meant less time off, but at my pay grade, I welcomed the overtime.

Agent Stanton and I drank our coffees while I gave him the shortened version of Agent Brown's death and all of the events surrounding it. When I finished talking, Agent Stanton shook his head in amazement, said I had done an outstanding job, and was very happy that I wanted to continue working with him, and he was honored to have such a great partner. I smiled and said, "Ditto."

"Let's go get your luggage and I'll give you a ride to your house," Agent Stanton said. I yawned, agreed, and we headed for baggage carousel number seven, lower level, terminal four.

"See you Monday morning," Agent Stanton said.

"Thanks again for coming to get me, especially on a Saturday. Say hi to Roberta for me, and I'll see you Monday." I waved, turned, and walked up the three brick stairs that led to my front door. Gosh, it was good to be home.

Tired, happy, and hungry, I decided to run first, get my mail second, stop at Trader Joe's for food third, and begin to get back on Pacific Standard Time. It was almost noon and I wanted to stay up until at least 7:00 p.m., so I had to keep myself busy for the rest of the afternoon.

June, July, and August were the busiest times at the beach, and watching cars cruise up and down my street, trying to snag a parking place, reminded me how thankful I was that I had a single-car garage with this apartment. It was such a joy to be home, back near the ocean. Its deep scent filling my nostrils, with waves and the sounds of laughter filling my ears, were exactly what I needed to begin unwinding. I ran for three miles, darting in and out of people on foot, skateboards, roller blades, and bicycles. I didn't mind; I was so content, running, feeling life flow through me, knowing how blessed I was to be home, and having such a great job and family. I made a mental note to call my sister and mom later and let them know I was home. They hadn't heard what had happened while I was gone, so we had a lot of catching up to do.

I decided to go to the store next to pick up a few things there; at the post office, I collected three weeks of mail. I didn't have to wonder anymore how I was going to stay up for the next couple of hours, for I had a stack of mail, flyers, and magazines that all needed to be sorted through.

I called my mom and my sister, and happily sorted through my mail for the rest of the day. I had a steak, red baked potato, and mixed green salad for dinner, along with a delicious glass of red wine, and tumbled into bed, falling asleep before my eyes even closed.

Sunday was spent doing laundry, getting out on the water with my kayak, going to Mass, and watching the evening news, and then *60 Minutes* before calling it a day. Jet lag didn't seem to affect me like it did when I came back from Asia, so I woke up the next morning refreshed and ready to get back to work at the CASFO.

As always, Agent Stanton was there when I walked in the door. Big Earl was there, too. We all talked for several minutes about our trips; unfortunately, mine had the most notoriety, with everyone who was in the office at some point over the next few days asking about the Agent Brown incident. My nickname changed from "Mad Dog" to "The Black Widow," but the new nickname was in such poor taste, even for federal law enforcement agents, that after a few days, I was back to being called "Mad Dog."

The reality of being back in the office hit me when I saw my in-box, or at least where it was supposed to be. I couldn't see it, for it was stacked with files and paperwork, the likes of which I'd never seen before. As Agent Stanton had told me on Saturday, just because you go on another assignment, it doesn't mean that the workload in the office stops; it just waits for your return.

Over the next few months I fell into the routine of copious amounts of overtime, airport, and air carrier inspections at my air-ports, opening civil penalty cases as needed when federal regulations were violated, conducting checkpoint testing, and happy hour each Friday at the Elephant Bar in Torrance to celebrate another week's end.

In September I traveled back to Marana, Arizona to attend the bi-annual recertification training that was now required. Another group of twenty-four agents spent a week qualifying in firearms proficiency, tactical training, fitness qualifications, and classroom workouts, learning self-defense techniques, knife takeaways, and classified security briefings. The training this week felt more relaxed, in that we knew what was expected of us, and we all had been training at various law enforcement ranges and fitness centers before returning to Marana. We were prepared to protect, and we all qualified for another six months.

My Jeep got me to and from Marana safely, and again I spent one night at my sister's on the way home. Precious time spent with my sister, my twin, my best friend. I was always so glad to see her.

The following week, again before quitting time on a Friday, Supervisor Drake called Agent Stanton, Big Earl, and me into his office to notify us that we had been scheduled for another air marshal mission. This time we were heading to Europe and were scheduled to leave in two weeks, which was the last full week of August.

"Be sure to have as much as possible of your case work, inspections, and checkpoint testing done before you travel. You'll all be gone for three weeks, so when you return you'll have only two weeks to complete everything that's open before the fiscal year ends. Performance appraisals and step increases are on the line if you don't get your work done," Supervisor Drake said in a very bland and matter-of-fact voice. "Enjoy your weekend; see you all on Monday." And with that, we were dismissed.

We, unlike Supervisor Drake, were elated. Another adventure was about to begin.

CHAPTER **TEN**

Flight Of Terror

OVERTIME WAS AN understatement. For the next two weeks we worked 65-hour weeks in an attempt to get everything done that we could. About midway through week two, reality — and the realization that we might not get everything done — hit us. Being fairly new to the organization, I wasn't sure what the implications of that meant just yet, but I had a strong suspicion I would find out if I didn't get my work completed.

The frustration on Supervisor Drake's face was unmistakable when Agent Stanton and I discussed our caseload, airport inspection activity, and checkpoint testing status with him the following morning. The two weeks of work, a blur of unending activity, was akin to running a marathon at knee-buckling speed, and still not winning the race, much less placing in it. Agent Stanton and I withstood the wrath of Supervisor Drake and his displeasure, when he kept yelling, "When the hell are you guys going to get your work done?"

But mostly the frustration came from the fact that Supervisor Drake had no control over our air marshal missions. When Washington, DC put a team together, you flew, unless there was a mighty good reason not to. And not having your written reports completed did not suffice as an excuse.

Agent Stanton and I finished up what we could on Friday, as did Big Earl, and we all headed home. Sunday morning, each of us would again be flying, this time to the Dallas Fort Worth International Airport (DFW) to meet the rest of the team members we would be flying with. Big Earl was flying to Dallas from Ontario Airport, since it was closer to his home. Agent Stanton and I were flying from LAX, but he had booked an early-morning flight, while I booked an afternoon flight because I wanted time to run in the morning. The team was scheduled to meet at the Dallas Fort Worth Field Office (DFW CASFO) located in Euless, Texas, a city on the airport perimeter. The hotel was in Bedford, the next city to the west of Euless, and from what I was told, the drive was short. Agent Stanton had rented a car in Dallas, so the three of us, and anyone else from our team, would have a car to use.

I was looking forward to this mission; another opportunity to fly as a marshal, with agents I knew, and to places I didn't know. I'd only been to England, so flying around Europe was going to be an adventure for me.

I got home, and settled into my usual weekend routine: running, cleaning, cooking, getting out on the water for a quick paddle in my yellow kayak, and getting to 5:00 p.m. Mass at Our Lady of Guadalupe Church. It was a whirlwind thirty-six hours, but my yellow suitcase was packed and standing by my door, waiting like a trusted dog in need of a walk — or in this case, in need of a flight. I was ready. "Okay, Maggie Stewart, here we go again."

With the checkpoint behind me, I realized that I had forgotten my book at home, so I wandered over to the airport magazine shop in terminal four to buy a book, bottle of water, and a pack of gum. I was hungry, so I got a bag of potato chips, too. "These are really good for you," I said to myself as I munched away, waiting for my flight to be called.

When my flight boarding was announced, I picked up my backpack, wiped my greasy potato chip fingers with a napkin, and headed for the gate. I was in an aisle seat, my favorite location, with only one seat next to me. I proceeded to board, found my seat, and took out my book again before I shoved my backpack underneath my seat. As everyone else boarded the flight, I quietly watched, listened, and kept my seatbelt unbuckled in case I needed to react.

The flight was almost completely full; I thought for a few minutes that I might be lucky enough to have an open seat beside me, but soon after, a gentleman in an airline uniform walked into the aircraft. I could tell that he was heading directly for the open seat next to mine.

The four-stripe applets told me he was a captain, but I didn't recognize the uniform. And as I predicted, he walked down the aisle, flight bag in hand, and said "Hello," while pointing to the window seat next to me. I stood up to allow him to get to his seat more easily, a tactic I learned quickly, after being unintentionally stepped on from time to time by clumsy passengers.

He was the last passenger to board, so the flight attendants quickly began the security briefings, checked for seatbelts and seat upright adherence, and walked quickly to their seats as the aircraft taxied for takeoff.

Once we were airborne, my seat neighbor introduced himself Captain Dave Smith. I introduced myself and we began our conversation of small talk about the weather and who we worked for, along with the usual checkpoint security screening horror stories. I found Dave to be interesting, engaging, and by the looks of his ringless left hand, unmarried.

The two and a half hour flight flew by; not a single page was turned in the book I had brought along, and as we taxied into the gate area at DFW, Dave asked if he could call me sometime.

I said, "Yes, but only if you're single."

Dave, smiled, took my hand, and said, "Yes, beautiful lady, I'm single." I immediately said yes and gave him my business card with my cell and home telephone numbers scribbled on the back. He too, gave me his number, which was an 817 area code, meaning he lived in Texas.

When we deplaned, we hugged, he kissed me on the cheek, and we went our separate ways — me to find the hotel shuttle, and he to connect on another flight to Raleigh-Durham, South Carolina, to catch up with his crew for his flight to Puerto Rico.

This might be all right. Here's a good-looking guy, an airline pilot, with tons of interesting stories, asking if he could call me, I thought smiling to myself. I hadn't been on too many dates since the Jerry surprise, a little over a year ago, so it might be time to get out and date again, even if he lived in Texas and I lived in California.

Dave worked for a cargo airline that flew mainly between the Caribbean, Miami, and Dallas Fort Worth. His routes didn't take him west to California, but he had flight privileges with all of the big cargo airlines — UPS, FEDEX, and Airborne Express — along with some of the major passenger airlines. So, I believed him when he said that if we wanted to see one another after this flight, there would be ways and opportunities to make that happen.

When I exited the American Airlines terminal on the upper level of DFW Airport, I was surprised by the stifling heat. I had forgotten how hot, humid, and sticky it could get in this part of the country. The wind was blowing my hair all around my face, and I wished I had put my sunglasses on before I exited the terminal. With bag in tow, I found a cab, and rode for fifteen minutes before arriving at my hotel, which was on the outskirts of the airport.

The hotel was small in comparison to many of the hotels that I had stayed at in the past year, but the staff was super friendly, the hotel lobby looked very modern, and there were freshly baked cookies at the checkout counter for the guests. Now that's my kind of hotel. And there was a happy hour from 5:00 p.m. to 7:00 p.m. as well.

Between meeting Dave, a great hotel, and an upcoming mission, I was feeling pretty darn sassy when I went outside for a run in the hot, windy city of Bedford.

I stayed closed to the hotel, as I always did, running around in circles, or straight lines, keeping the hotel in sight, until I gained my bearings. Since I didn't normally run with anyone, safety in numbers wasn't an option, so safety in sight became my motto. My skin immediately became wet and sticky as I ran, watching the afternoon clouds building into huge hammerheads, meaning rain, thunder, and lightning were likely in the near future. Running here was a whole lot different from running in Southern California, so I continued to watch the beautiful skies of Texas fill with clouds, with small gusts of wind, indicating a front was moving in. It was time for this girl to turn and head for the hotel.

With the first spits of warm rain beginning to fall, I jogged up to the hotel, and walked into the lobby to see Agent Stanton and Big Earl sitting at the bar. I waved, calling out, "Hi guys, I'll be down in a few minutes. I just need to change."

"Okay, we'll have a glass of wine waiting for you, Maggie," Big Earl shouted back.

Happy hour here was a meal: chicken wings that were hotter than I'd ever tasted, smothered in spicy red sauce; celery, carrots, chips, salsa, small meat sandwiches, and popcorn. Wine, beer, and well drinks were one dollar. No wonder everyone on our team was here feasting away.

True to Big Earl's word, my glass of chardonnay was already there. So all I had to do was fill my plate with tasty treats, and settle in at the bar between Big Earl and an agent I didn't know. "Hello, I'm Maggie Stewart. I'm from the LAX CASFO."

"Hi, I'm Randy, from St. Louis," he said as we shook hands.

Big Earl began telling me who was flying this trip, but I knew only Agent Stanton and Big Earl. The rest of the team was a combination of "old timers," meaning agents that were hired in the first air marshal class, and the "newbies" from the third and fourth classes. Big Earl and I were hired in the second class. I was looking forward to meeting everyone tomorrow during our intelligence briefing.

After my second glass of wine and another bowl of popcorn, I decided that I'd better call it a day, and headed for my room. I stopped at the small self-service gift shop, selecting three postcards to send to my mom, brother, and sister, a tradition I started years ago, back then, as now, a link to home, to family, to my world. I never wrote much, letting the picture on the postcard speak for itself, but at least my family knew where I had been, and that I loved them.

The following morning, gathering in the hotel lobby, I noticed that a few of my teammates might have indulged in the happy hour more than they probably wished at 0700 hours. I dropped my postcard in the outgoing mailbox at the front desk, wandered over to the group, and said good morning.

At the office the day was spent getting documents in order, listening to intelligence briefings, and getting to know our team members better. Again, I was the only female on this trip, so I planned mentally once again to spend my downtime with Agent Stanton or Big Earl. The team leader, Agent Mike Whiskers, was from headquarters and had been with the agency for five years, transitioning into the air marshal program a few years ago. He was a former intelligence analyst with the Army, so his security briefings were in-depth, full of details and side notes about the countries' cultures and terrorist activities. The two-hour briefing covered the five countries — Germany, France, Spain, Italy, and India — that our team would be flying in and out of. Mike, as he asked to be called, advised us that we were scheduled to depart tomorrow morning at 0725 on American Airlines for the fifteen-hour flight to Frankfurt, Germany.

Back at the hotel, I decided to pass on happy hour, opting to go for a long run, pack, and then tumble into bed by 9:00 p.m. – that was my goal. My Sandhill Crane alarm was set to wake me at 0330 hours. Our team needed to be at the airport by 0530.

By the time we landed in Frankfurt I wasn't sure if I was coming or going. I was exhausted. Staying awake for the fifteen hour and ten minute flight turned out to be one of the most challenging things I have ever done. It was grueling to watch people sleep, dozing off...with their heads bobbing from side to side, trying to seek comfort, while seated in the most uncomfortable seats ever designed. Fortunately, I was in coach, all the way aft in the B-747, so I could cover my zone while standing, directly behind my last row seat, adjacent to the lavatories. Agent Jimmy Sparks was seated in the last row directly across from me, so we both rotated between standing and being seated for the entire flight, while watching over our flock of 400-plus passengers, in the three-class design aircraft. We had to worry about only a portion of coach, but in reality, you worry about everything when you're on duty.

After we deplaned, we waited while our team leader Mike coordinated all of our in-country processes, each one of us stretching, yawning, our bodies screaming for sleep. But for now, we had to wait.

The Sheraton Frankfurt Airport Hotel would be our haven today. Most of the flights we would be flying over the next three weeks departed and arrived in the late-evening hours. Today was the beginning of a series of flying, sleeping, eating, and repeating the sequence all over again. Many of the flights departed within twenty-four hours of one another, so ground time, and rest, would be luxuries during this mission. We would be seeing the lobby of this Sheraton many times this trip, since we had multiple layovers in Frankfurt.

After I checked in, I ordered room service, unpacked my night clothes, and put out the clothes I was going to need tomorrow. Tomorrow we were flying to Barcelona, Spain — again, with less than twenty-four hours on the ground before returning back here to Frankfurt.

A hotel employee delivered my meal, thanked me in perfect English for the tip I gave her, and said to enjoy my meal and stay here. I ate quickly since I hadn't eaten much on the airplane, showered, and then slept for nearly ten hours before waking up, momentarily startled because I didn't know where I was.

Packed and ready, I went downstairs to check out, get something to eat, and be ready to leave for the airport at 1300 hours for our two-hour flight to Barcelona. The flight was scheduled to leave at 1600 hours.

The Renaissance Barcelona Airport Hotel was our layover destination, again with no ground time to see anything other than the view from the very short ride to and from the airport to the hotel.

When we arrived back in Frankfurt the following afternoon, again we'd have less than twenty-four hours before departing for Rome,

Italy. We were scheduled for one full day off in Rome, and we were all looking forward to the time off and the opportunity to see some of the sights.

The following evening we departed for Rome at 2155 hours and flew for one hour and forty-five minutes. After clearing customs and checking in with the law enforcement agency at the airport, our workday finished, and at 0200 hours, we all piled into cabs for the short ride to the La Residenza Hotel. While checking in, a few of us agreed to meet later that day, at 11:00 a.m., to do some sightseeing while we had the opportunity.

I set my alarm for 8:30 a.m. I felt the pressures of the day begin slipping away as I closed my eyes. Thanking the Lord for a safe trip, and hoping to have a date with Dave sometime in the near future, I fell into a sound sleep.

Four of us — Agent Stanton, Big Earl, Jimmy Sparks, and I — met in the lobby at 11:00 a.m. as planned. The four-star La Residenza Hotel was beautiful, with its sophisticated style, and was located in the heart of the historic center of Rome. The bell clerk told us that we could walk to the Spanish Steps, the Trevi Fountain, the Piazza, and the US Embassy. He pointed the way, hands flailing, while his facial expressions showed the passion he felt for the city he lived in.

We set off on our adventure: to find the US Embassy first, and food second, and some sightseeing third. It was a glorious day; the sun shone brightly, and people in brightly colored clothing — orange, pink, green, and purple — filled the sidewalks. Voices rose above the car engines and the buzz of shop owners selling their various goods and services. And the scents of the small cafés we passed almost brought me to my knees. I was hungry.

Brussels, Rome, and Paris all had international security field offices located in the US Embassy. During our intelligence briefings, it was always recommended that a courtesy visit to the field office occur while visiting any of those cities, because the resident agent there might have information for the team that was not provided by the staff back in Washington, DC.

After a few wrong turns, we found the embassy, presented our credentials, and were given directions to the security office located on the third floor. The resident agent, Agent Bones, was available to see us; in fact, he insisted that we all walk to his favorite pizzeria for lunch.

No one had to ask me twice. "I'm in," I said, as everyone else nodded in agreement.

We walked a few blocks to a small pizzeria with outdoor seating, and we found a table that seated five. A waiter appeared, handed us all menus which Agent Bones began interpreting for us. He recommended that we order several pizzas and the brochette for an appetizer. We all agreed, the order was placed, and we settled in to people-watch, basking in the warm sun, and discussing what was going on back in Washington, and other parts of the country. Agent Bones had been away from the United States for the past five years, and was very interested in hearing all of the news, from sports and politics to fashion. He hung on our every word. *Who is giving whom a briefing?* I thought, and smiled.

When the meal arrived, the beauty of it surprised me. Large plates of thin-crusted pizza, with vivid colors of various vegetables adorning the platter, as the vivid colors of people's clothing earlier had dotted the streets. The brochette was plump and red, with parsley, chopped garlic, and garlic bread to place the brochette on when eating. It was a magical feast that I couldn't wait to try. We all dug in with gusto, and the meal was as delicious as it was beautiful. I had never had brochette before; I now knew I would have it many more times in the future. What a delicious meal.

We said our farewells to Agent Bones at the restaurant. He needed to get back to the office, and everyone else wanted to sightsee. Stuffed and content, we began our self-guided tour of this beautiful city. We stopped at the Spanish Steps, following the steep 138-step climb between the Piazza di Spagna at the base, and the Piazza Trinita dei Monti church at the top. When we walked back down the steps, heading toward the Trevi Fountain, we were surprised, and disappointed, to see a McDonalds within blocks of the Spanish Steps.

The three of us wanted to see the Trevi Fountain. When we got to the fountain, Big Earl said, "This was the theme of the 1954 movie *Three Coins in the Fountain* and the Academy Award-winning song by the same name. Believe it or not, there it's estimated that over 3,000 coins are thrown into this fountain every day. The money is used to help the needy." The Roman fountain was more beautiful than I could have imagined. Before leaving, each of us threw a coin into the fountain; legend had it that if you throw a coin, you are assured to return to Rome.

We sat, basking in the sun, among the locals, tourists, and occasional pickpocket, who wanted to lift our wallets to make a quick buck. But we saw only fountains, birds, and felt the rays of glorious sunshine warming our faces, as we sat in this famous city square.

When the three of us arrived back at the hotel several hours later, our feet were tired and we all had slight sunburns, but we were very appreciative to have had a few hours to tour this beautiful city.

The following morning, retracing our footsteps back to the airport, we again flew from Rome to Frankfurt, to reposition for our flight to Bombay leaving the following afternoon at 1:35 p.m. This would be the longest leg of this mission, an eight hour and thirty minute trip aboard a Pan Am B-747.

I was fortunate to be seated in first class for the long flight from Frankfurt to Bombay. I was seated next to a woman who talked non-stop, her hands moving as she spoke. She was American, and her husband was the captain on this flight, she told me, without taking one breath. "Great," I said, as we chatted about India and all the other places she had flown with her husband, who was retiring next year after twenty-five years with Pan Am. This was his final trip internationally, so he had made special arrangements with the airline to accommodate his wish that his wife accompany him. *What an opportunity*, I thought; then I smiled, because I was doing the same thing, but getting paid.

I knew that reading was not going to be an option on this flight, at least, for as long the captain's wife was awake. I learned that she and her husband had traveled all over the world, and they had come to India many times before. As she spoke, she bobbed her head, her short gray-blonde hair also bobbing, her big brown eyes widening at every new sentence. She was a hoot! So vivid, alive, and excited about every opportunity she had been afforded.

About five hours into the flight, the captain's voice interrupted our conversation to advise the passengers that we were beginning to get into some weather, advising everyone to keep their seatbelts fastened while seated, and that the food service was going to be delayed until they were on the other side of the weather system.

The captain's wife, Linda, and I looked at one another, and she began talking once again. Over the next thirty minutes, the aircraft began to rock and roll, as I called it, dipping and bowing as she sped across the Indian Ocean toward India.

All of a sudden, the aircraft lights flickered off, and then on, then off again, as the aircraft rapidly dropped. Every overhead bin opened, dropping their contents on the passengers, and as the oxygen masks deployed, the passengers began screaming and shouting. The airplane, jarred from side to side, started gaining and losing altitude, while lightning from the thunderstorm raged outside, its long tentacles of power trying to get inside and cause us harm. Linda grabbed my arm, and began screaming. She was terrified, and so was I, as we watched the aircraft walls buckle in the fierce turbulence of the storm.

I don't know how long we were in the storm, but eventually, thankfully, we escaped with our lives, and as the aircraft stabilized, the screams became silent, replaced with clapping and shouts of "praise God."

The captain came back on the P.A. system, saying that everything was okay from the cockpit, and the flight attendants would be in the cabin shortly to check on everyone. But for now, he wanted everyone to remain seated, until we were completely out of the clouds we had just flown through.

Linda unclenched her fingers from my left wrist, laid her head back, closed her eyes, and I suspect, prayed for a few minutes. I looked around, and behind me I could see a couple of the other air marshals on board, who gave me a thumbs up, indicating that they were all right, and their areas secure. "This flight of terror is secure," I said, half to myself and half out loud. "Good God, Maggie Stewart, what a ride."

About thirty minutes later the captain came out of the cockpit, walked over to our seats, and began speaking with his wife, asking how she was, and then turned to me to ask how I was doing, and what the status of the rest of our team was. Linda, turned, looking at me, then back at her husband, with a question mark chiseled firmly on her face. The captain immediately understood that he had just jeopardized my cover, apologized, kissed his wife, and proceeded to walk through the cabin checking on the crew and the passengers.

"I'll tell you my story after we land, OK? But for now, consider me a fellow traveler," I whispered.

Unfazed Linda said, "Oh, OK," and we talked for the remaining two hours of the flight, mostly about the incident we had just survived, their children back home in Houston, Texas, and what they were going to do while they were in India.

As we landed at Bombay International Airport, I could see fire trucks stationed on both sides of the runway. I could only assume that the captain had radioed ahead, explained our rough encounter with turbulence, and made the decision to have emergency crews meet the flight as a precautionary measure. After the rough ride, I have to admit, I didn't blame him.

Fortunately, the landing gear had not been damaged, and we landed without incident. Our plane was parked in a remote area of the airfield, away from the terminal. The passengers deplaned and were transported to the terminal on large buses. The flight crew, our team of air marshals, and the captain's wife remained onboard. Once all of the buses were well on their way to the terminal, the captain asked all of us to come take a look at the aircraft.

The captain began explaining, pointing, and gesturing for us to look up at the nose of the aircraft. We all craned our necks, looking up at the nose cone, which had multiple visible holes punched in the gray cover that protected the front of the aircraft. "See those holes?" asked the captain. "Those were all caused by multiple lightning strikes," he said. "We're damn lucky we didn't lose the cockpit windshield. If you thought it was a wild ride in the back, you should have seen it from up front," he said with a grim expression. "We parked out here, away from the terminal, because this bird is grounded. We'll be here for a few days, I suspect, until a replacement aircraft can be flown in."

Agent Whiskers, our team leader, nodded as well, knowing that he was going to be on the telephone for a while this evening, discussing the day's events with DC, and waiting for them to come up with another plan for his team.

A few minutes later, carry-ons in hand, we all boarded the waiting bus, which would take us to the terminal. I sat behind the captain and his wife for the short ride. We knew we were all staying at the same hotel, and we made arrangements to meet for dinner later that evening.

The Westin Garden City was another very modern, American-looking hotel in every respect. The hotel lobby was gorgeous, and the immediate personal attention received from the staff was overwhelming, yet welcome at the same time. Most of us were exhausted, and we agreed to have an early dinner in the hotel's lavish restaurant. The captain, his wife, Big Earl, Agent Sparks, and I decided to meet in the lobby at 6:00 p.m.

My room was on the tenth floor. After riding from the airport to the hotel in a cab, I knew I was not going to run outdoors, due to the masses of people — children, mostly — that surrounded us before we got into our cab. Again, just prior to the walled entrance to the hotel, children were everywhere shouting— touching the cab, begging for money. As I looked out my tenth-floor window I could see that we were walled in, the ten-plus-foot walls dividing the hotel guests from the ghettos and the terrible living conditions just a few feet away.

Part of our original security briefing included instructions to stay at the hotel during our layover, to not drink any tap water, or eat any fruits or vegetables that were not served at the hotel. During that briefing, and now from what I saw directly below my window, I was convinced that it was best to eat in the hotel.

I had learned to run stairs in the hotels where I couldn't run outside either for weather, pollution, or safety reasons. There were fifteen stories in this hotel, so there were plenty of stairwells to run, safely, up and down, again and again. I changed clothes and found my way to the stairs, going down and then back up, legs aching and my lungs screaming, until I was calm and smiling once again. There's nothing like a good run to get the post-mission adrenaline out of you.

Agent Sparks, Big Earl, the captain, and his wife were waiting for me when in the lobby at 6:00 p.m. I was a few minutes late and I apologized profusely for keeping them waiting while we walked to the main dining room. The service and food were superb. We dined on tender curry-flavored meats, rice, vegetables rich in color (and, I hoped, thoroughly washed). During dinner, Agents Sparks showed us the video he had taken during the flight. Captain Martin said he was still impressed that we escaped with our lives. He had spoken to flight operations since we last saw him, and the manager on duty had apologized. The meteorologist on duty didn't know the magnitude of the storm, or, obviously the instability of the air and subsequent wind shears, when air traffic, along with airline flight operations, authorized us to fly through the bank of cumulonimbus clouds. Captain Martin said that sometimes that happens — weather forecasting isn't an exact science — but at least everything turned out well.

Captain Martin told us that a replacement plane would arrive in two days, and that he had already advised our team leader. Captain Martin and Linda were going to Elephanta Island tomorrow and invited us to join them. He said they'd already made travel arrangements for the ride to the ferry, that there was plenty of room, and if we were interested, to be in the lobby tomorrow at 10:00 a.m. We thanked them, saying we'd know more tomorrow after our 8:00 a.m. scheduled team meeting.

In our case, as luck would have it, the next morning Agent Whiskers advised us that we would have the next two days off. We were scheduled to depart for Frankfurt at 9:00 a.m. on Friday. "If you elect to go outside the hotel, stick together, watch your wallets, and watch what you eat and drink. This is a beautiful country, unfortunately riddled with poverty; each of you will immediately be recognized as either Canadian or American, and the begging will commence." We were dismissed.

I met Captain Martin and Linda in the lobby at 10:00 a.m. Big Earl, Agent Sparks, and the rest of the team elected to do other things.

The ferry ride took about an hour, leaving from the harbor, or the "Gateway of India," as they called it here. The ride cost about seven US dollars for a "luxury boat" that had an upper deck. I think the only luxurious thing about this boat was the upper deck, but I was content to be with two people who were fast becoming my friends.

On the ferry ride, Captain Martin told me that Elephanta Island was a very popular tourist destination for a day trip because of its cave temples, the Elephanta Caves, which had been carved out of rock. The island has about 1200 people living here, growing rice to make a living, among the thickly wooded palms, mango, and tamarind trees. "And don't be alarmed by the small monkeys that run amok here, playing, and stealing items on occasion," Captain Martin said with a smile.

When we got back to the hotel we decided to venture out again tomorrow, meeting at 10:00 a.m. in the lobby, this time to tour the city. It turned out that Captain Martin and Linda had been here numerous times, enjoying antiques shopping, and of course giving the local children surprises. I wondered what he meant by "surprises," but I knew I'd find out tomorrow.

The next day, when we met in the hotel lobby, Captain Martin was carrying a large white mesh sack with him. It was filled to the brim with small writing pads, pens, pencils, and small rubber balls. When I inquired about the unique day pack, Captain Martin laughed and began explaining that instead of giving money to the begging children that surrounded you immediately every time you went outdoors, that he gave them something from his mesh bag. It wasn't money, which was usually collected for the parents, the children not always seeing any benefit, but this was something they could have for themselves. It was their own toy, something most adults didn't want, so the child was able to keep it. Captain Martin and his wife had been handing out these small gifts for years; it was one of the many things that they would miss doing when he retired next year.

We left the hotel to go antique shopping, looking at small and large treasures alike. I purchased a small lock made of brass, shaped like a lion with its tail curling over its back, sticking into the back of its head, and out the front to form the lock. The key was inserted at the base of the lion's feet and if done correctly, would release the tail from the lion's mouth, opening the lock. It was one of the most unique locks I had ever seen. It was small, and a practical memento for me to carry home. The captain and his wife didn't buy anything, but they handed out an enormous number of "surprises" to the children.

I had grown to greatly admire Captain Martin these past few days, not only for saving all of our lives, but also for showing such hospitality to our team, as if this country were his personal home, and it was his duty to make sure we were comfortable. But this act of giving was by far the kindest and most humanitarian gesture I had ever seen.

The next morning, we all grabbed cabs at 0530 for the ride back to the airport, our long layover in India coming to a close. Captain Martin, Linda, and I had exchanged personal addresses the night before in case we didn't have time to talk today. I discovered that was smart of us, since I was seated in coach, Linda in first class, and of course Captain Martin was flying left seat in the cockpit.

The flight was long, tedious, and full of people moving about, stirring in their seats, walking up and down the aisles, and in and out of the lavatories, as everyone tried to get comfortable on the nine-hour flight to Frankfurt.

Our flight schedule was off-track, delayed by three days, so for the next five days, we flew a relentless schedule between Frankfurt, Paris, Spain, and back to Frankfurt, before boarding our flight from Frankfurt to Dallas on the sixth day.

Our three-week mission was almost complete, with one more sixteen-hour flight to go, an eight-hour layover in Dallas, and then back to Los Angeles.

My second mission was almost complete. I'd made new friends, seen another part of the world, and continued to protect those sleepy, impatient, and unknowing passengers that surrounded me. This was an incredible job — I loved it, and I was one kick-ass woman.

CHAPTER ELEVEN

Standing Guard

I WAS ECSTATIC to be home. I felt like a cliff swallow, returning home to California in the pre-dawn hours, to rebuild my nest, soon to rejoin my flock at the office, and my community that I was growing to cherish. I had roamed widely, like the swallow, these past months, and now I was ready to stay in one place, exploring the beaches of Redondo, Hermosa, and Manhattan, finding new places to kayak, run, and have some fun.

I unpacked my yellow suitcase, put it in my closet, and lay down to take a nap for a few hours. I made a mental note of all the things that I needed to do, but "Later," I said to myself. "Later; right now I need a few hours of sleep."

When I woke three hours later, it was still early, 9:00 a.m. on a Saturday, so I had the weekend to relax and catch up. I called my sister, knowing she'd be up, and we talked about everything that had been going on over the past month or so, with her, her family, and my mom. I hadn't called my mom or my brother in several months, so I made a mental note to call them this weekend too.

After my sister and I hung up, I decided it was time to go for a run, stop at Trader Joe's for food, and then get my mail. These tasks, in this order, had become my usual post-flight activities, so when I left my house I knew exactly where I was going, and how long it would take.

With my usual three-mile run done, I stopped and picked up a few necessities at the store, then walked the two short blocks to the post office. The post office wasn't crowded, with only one other customer at the counter in front of me. I stopped behind the yellow line on the floor, put my brown Trader Joe's grocery bag down, and waited my turn. This annex post office was very small, with only two counters for customer service, and was nestled in a book or gift store type of business. There were rows of post office rental boxes lining one wall, and racks of book and gift items lining the opposite wall. I wasn't sure if this was originally a post office or a store, but somehow over the years, the two merged together. It was one of the most unique post offices I had ever seen. I was grateful that it was here, since it was within walking distance of my beach cottage.

When it was my turn, I let the clerk know that I needed to pick up my mail after being gone for a little over three weeks. She asked for my address, and then went into the back office. When she returned, the stack of mail she gave me was a combination of magazines, junk mail, and regular-sized envelopes. I immediately wished I had gotten another shopping bag when I was at the grocery store. The clerk, sensing my need, reached down beneath the counter and came up with a plastic shopping bag for me. "I just happen to have an extra one, if you would like it," she said.

"Gosh, thank you," I said. As I walked home I marveled at the kindness of people.

Just as I put my key in the door, my neighbor Bill stopped by to say hello. He was on his bicycle, heading to lunch with friends. He said he was glad I was home, and laughed at his own words, that I was the quietest neighbor he had ever had. I smiled, waved goodbye and watched him ride down Camino Del La Costa toward Hermosa Beach.

I dropped my bags on the kitchen table, put the groceries away, poured a glass of orange juice, sorted quickly through the mail, and to my delight, found two postcards: one mailed from Miami, the second mailed from Puerto Rico, and both from Dave Smith, the captain I had met on my flight from Los Angeles to Dallas three weeks earlier.

I went outside, sat on my brick steps leading into my cottage, set my glass of orange juice beside me, and quickly read Dave's cards. His writing style was block printing — not neat, not sloppy, and written in blue ink, with the circle of the o's and a's not completing closing as he wrote. He said how nice it was to have met me, and he hoped we'd meet again soon. He signed each card "Captain Dave." What a surprise. I was grinning ear to ear, when the other Bill in our apartment complex zoomed down his stairs. He quickly said, "Hello."

"Hi." My greeting barely escaped my lips as he dashed to his garage, started his car, and squealed out the driveway. "Wow, he's in a hurry today."

I finished up my orange juice, went back inside, put the postcards in the window above my sink, tilted my head, smiled, and decided I'd better get some laundry done. I had wanted to call Dave on my eight-hour layover in Dallas yesterday, but I was so tired, along with being short on time, that I decided to wait until I got home. Now I had a very good reason to call: a thank you was without a doubt in order.

With my laundry in piles, one load of whites already tumbling away, I again went back outside, sat on my back steps, and dialed Dave's number. The telephone rang four times before the answering machine picked up. "This is Captain Dave, I can't get to the phone right now, so please leave your name and number, and I will call you back."

"Hi, this is Maggie Stewart. I'm back from my trip. Thanks for the postcards. Call me back when you can. Bye for now." I placed the phone back in its cradle and with a sigh thought, *Well, what should I do next?*

I spent the rest of the day cleaning up, reading my mail, and getting my little cottage back in order. As sunset neared, I put a glass of chardonnay in a plastic cup, and walked one block down to the beach, arriving a few minutes before the big red fiery ball slipped beneath the sea to awaken another part of the world. It was still warm, and school was back in for most of the children in this area. But I was always amazed, with the population as large as Redondo Beach had, that more people weren't out watching the sun go down every evening. Walking down to the beach and watching the sunset had become a tradition of mine almost immediately after moving to the Esplanade. A glass of wine, a sunset, and the ocean — it just couldn't get any better than that. *Well, almost couldn't get any better. A special man to share this time with would make it better*, I thought to myself.

I walked back to the house, deciding to cook a rib-eye steak, baked potato, and salad for dinner. I hadn't had a good steak in a while, so I was ready to gorge myself. I'd have to run more miles tomorrow, but right now, I didn't care; I just wanted to eat a delicious, fattening, home-cooked meal.

I got the barbecue started, threw a potato in the microwave, and made a simple salad with romaine lettuce, tomato, avocado, and croutons. I marinated the steak and cooked it for seven minutes on each side, keeping it medium rare. "Just perfect," I said out loud, as I walked back into the house, placed the potato on my plate beside the steak, and headed for the sofa. I rarely ate at the table, a habit I picked up long ago. When eating alone, I felt more comfortable eating more casually. I sat down, and dug in.

Just as I was putting my dishes in the sink, the telephone rang; I hoped it was Dave calling me back. "Hello," I said.

"Hi, this is Captain Dave, calling you back. How are you, Maggie?"

Again, we talked for hours, about our trips, our lives, our youth, favorite sports teams, on and on, long into the night. At midnight, we said our goodbyes, and made an agreement to talk again tomorrow. Dave said he was home until Tuesday when his next trip started, taking him this time to North Carolina, Florida, and Puerto Rico again. He'd be gone for a week.

"Okay — night Dave, I'll talk to you tomorrow then. Bye," I said, and we both reluctantly hung up our telephones.

When I opened my sleepy eyes Sunday morning, I could see the rays of morning sunshine seeping through my window, streaming down on my bed, like a blanket of joy. I felt very joyful this morning, full of hope, full of dreams, and fully ready to go for a long run.

I had decided a few months ago that I wanted to start training to run a marathon. I had recently read a book by Jeff Galloway, *Galloway's Book on Running*. Jeff Galloway was on the US Olympic team for track in 1972, and had set an American record in the 10-mile. His book discussed everything, from the physiology of running, to diet, injuries, training schedules, and shoes. I had never run in any competitive races since track in elementary school, and certainly not these types of distances, but I had made up my mind that I wanted to run 26.2 miles, and I was going for it.

My best friend since elementary school, Ruthy Globus, had a husband who was a distance runner, so when I called her, telling her what I wanted to do, her husband suggested I get this book, read it, and then map out a plan. Well, I'd read the book and mapped out a plan, but hadn't had time to execute that plan until now. The basic training plan I would be following from Galloway's book outlined a 32-week schedule and I was on week three, since I was already running three miles for my longest distance.

Each Sunday I would increase my long runs by one mile. When I reached ten miles, I would increase my mileage by one mile every other week until I reached twenty-six miles. It was an easy plan to follow, but the hardest part would be carving out the time each Sunday, running farther and farther until race day. I wanted to run the Palos Verdes Marathon next year in May, which meant I needed to start training today. Since I'd been on so much travel, I decided to run three miles today, and increase my mileage weekly from now on.

I made a pot of coffee, got my running gear on, grabbed half a bagel, spread a little bit of peanut butter on it, and stepped out the door into the morning sunshine. I walked to the corner to warm up, and began running, feeling marvelous from being outside, talking to Dave last night, and living in such a perfect place.

Returning from my run, I quickly changed, rushing out the door again, faster this time, because I didn't want to be late for Mass, which began at 11:30 a.m. It was 11:15, so I was cutting it close, but a good Catholic is occasionally late — at least, that's what a friend of mine used to tell me. I never liked to be late for church, especially at Our Lady of Guadalupe. The choir was superb, and their voices were rich, vibrant, and full of the Holy Spirit. I loved sitting quietly, listening, and reflecting on what I needed to talk with God about that day. Church, like running, was my place and time to refuel.

I parked a few blocks away, and managed to slip in the side door just as Father Ray was beginning Mass. I quickly dipped two fingers into the holy water, made the sign of the cross, quietly found a pew that had an open seat on the end, and sat down, breathing a sigh of relief. I wasn't late; I had missed the music, but I wouldn't miss the service.

After Mass, on my way home, I stopped at the store, picking up a few items that I had forgotten on Saturday, and headed back home. I needed to start getting organized for tomorrow, and clean up some paperwork on my desk, pay some bills, and call my mom and my brother. I hoped that Dave would call too.

"Sandhill Crane alarm, go away," I said out loud at 5:00 Monday morning. I knew I couldn't afford to hit the snooze alarm; I needed every minute in the next hour to get dressed, out the door, and be at the office by 6:00 a.m. I had stayed up too late talking to my mom, my brother, and then Dave last night. By the time Dave and I hung up, it was 11:00 p.m. I knew, last night, that this morning I was going to be cranky, but I didn't care then, and we talked for a couple of hours, like we had the night before.

When I walked in the office, Agent Stanton was standing in the middle of the room, coffee cup brimful of hot steamy coffee, as he nodded a greeting. Kelly and Big Earl were the only other people in the office. It was just a few minutes before 6:00; I was on time, and ready to tackle my travel voucher and the enormous pile of paperwork that I knew, without any doubt, had accumulated in my in-box over the past few weeks. I was used to all the paperwork by now, knowing, that no matter where you were — training, international travel, or air marshal missions — the paperwork never stopped. It didn't follow you around the world, but it waited stealthily, sleeping in your in-box until your return, and its eventual awakening to be dealt with. I'd never seen so much paperwork in my life; I had always heard that the government was known for its abundance of paperwork, but now I knew first hand.

Once I had my first cup of coffee in hand, Agent Stanton, Big Earl, Kelly, and I caught up on the office politics. Big Earl and I listened for the most part, since the two of us had been away. The only really juicy news was that Supervisor Drake had applied for a position at the regional office, and if he got promoted, there would be an opening here at this office for a first-line supervisor's position. No one could speak to who might actually apply for the position, but we were all very good at conjecture, keeping the rumor mill going at this point. Once we were done, it was time to start going through the paperwork that I could clearly see piled high on my desk. Big Earl's desk was a mess too! We both shrugged our shoulders, and headed to our desks to dig in for the day. Agent Stanton and I talked about our testing and inspection schedule, deciding that today I should stay at the office, get my voucher done, prioritize my cases, and deal with other correspondence that was on my desk. Sure sounded like a good idea to me. Agent Stanton was going to head over to Burbank Airport and do some checkpoint testing on his own, so he would be gone most of the day.

It took me two days to get my voucher completed, and my desk organized enough to venture out to my airports. Unfortunately, while at LAX, I found one door unsecured, and had two checkpoint test failures. By mid-week, my first week back in the office, I had added three more cases to my workload. "Well, here's hoping I can stay home the rest of the year," I said to Agent Stanton before I left the office on Wednesday. "I doubt that will happen," he said. "But I'll keep my fingers crossed for you, kiddo."

Three weeks passed; summer was fading into winter, daylight hours were dwindling, and my Sunday-morning runs were chillier. I still wore shorts, but with a sweatshirt, and a wool cap to keep my ears warm. I was up to six miles now, and feeling great.

Dave and I continued to talk every day on the telephone; he had flown one trip to the Caribbean, another to North Carolina, and was heading to Houston tomorrow for a couple of days, and then he'd have five days off. We talked about meeting in Las Vegas next weekend, after his trip, for a long weekend, in a neutral place that was both fun and inexpensive. I could drive there from Redondo Beach in about five hours, and Dave could fly from Dallas in about two hours. I was excited; a plan was coming together, and I was looking forward to seeing Dave again. We mapped out a plan to travel and meet late Thursday, hang out Friday and Saturday, and travel again on Sunday. I said I'd find the hotel, and Dave said he'd make travel arrangements.

I had earned some travel compensation time that needed to be used before the end of the calendar year, or I was going to lose it. "Use or Lose" is vacation time, or leave as we call it in the government, which accumulates when you travel outside of your normal work schedule. You can keep it for a certain period of time, and if you don't use it, you lose it.

On Monday morning, I filled out my leave slip for Thursday and Friday, and placed it on Kelly's desk, so she could pass it along to Supervisor Drake. With only three days to work this week, I mentally mapped out the priorities again, so nothing would be missed.

When I came back from lunch, in top of my in-box was my approved leave slip from Supervisor Drake. Happily, I penciled the time off in my planner, making a mental note to call Dave later.

The next few days flew by. I completed several civil penalty cases that I had opened during the past few months, and attended two monthly meetings at LAX with Agent Stanton; one was the monthly security airport meeting, the second a meeting with the international carriers to discuss the status of the additional security measures that had been implemented, and if any vulnerabilities had been noted by the carriers. In many cases, airline employees were the best security eyes and ears for law enforcement and the federal government because they knew their operations better than anyone else.

If something was suspicious, or out of the norm, many times airline employees discovered it first.

Agent Stanton attended every security meeting he possibly could at his airports, because visibility built rapport, better lines of communications, and the sense of being a team, rather than adversaries. In my opinion, this was sage advice, and I intended to follow in Agent Stanton's footsteps by following his advice at my airports, too.

Come Monday morning, walking into the office I was on cloud nine. My Vegas weekend was behind me, my in-box didn't look like I'd taken extra days off, and I didn't think I had any new cases assigned to me. Kelly smiled, waved me over to her desk, and asked, "So, what's the scoop, girl?"

"We had a wonderful time; he's really, really nice, Kelly. I like this guy; we walked, talked, gambled, went to a couple of shows, and well, we had a really good time," I said with the biggest grin on my face. "We definitely like each other."

"Awesome. It's about time you found someone you like," Kelly said.

After lunch, Supervisor Drake hollered out his office door for Agent Stanton and me to come to his office. That was just his way; he never got up from his desk; he never used the intercom system on the telephones; he just hollered. The first time he hollered, a year or so ago, I nearly jumped out of my skin, but now I just went to find out what he was yelling about.

"Get ready to pack your bags again, you two," Drake said. "You're off to Miami next Monday for another mission. This is last-minute, shorter than most trips; you will be gone only about ten days. There's a telecom scheduled for 10:00 tomorrow morning. That's it; now get back to work."

At ten the next morning, we learned that we would travel Sunday, and then begin flying daily trips to Haiti. The details would be discussed at our first team briefing, scheduled for 0800 on Monday. We were told this threat was specific, teams had already been deployed, and we were part of the continuous coverage for flights in and out of Haiti.

I hadn't been to Miami in years; I had forgotten how humid it gets, even in the fall. Agent Stanton and I took the same flight from Los Angeles to Miami, collected our luggage from the baggage carousel, and took the hotel shuttle to the Miami International Hotel, located within the MIA International Terminal at the airport. We arrived at the hotel within minutes after stepping onto the shuttle.

While I was checking in, the guest service agent advised me that all of the rooms were soundproof; four restaurants were located in the hotel, with the main restaurant having not only four-star food, but an excellent view of the airport; an indoor swimming pool and a first-class fitness facility were located on the top floor. I took special note of these amenities, because I suspected there wouldn't be much time to run outdoors on this mission. I silently thanked myself for having the forethought to bring a swimsuit too.

My room was bland tan, yellow, and beige, and my "excellent" view was the first floor mezzanine roof, complete with heating and air conditioning units, the machinery of necessity. Thankfully the rooms really were soundproof. Sadly for me, I was facing away from the airport — no view of the taxiing aircraft, either.

I changed into my swimsuit and decided to swim before going in search of dinner. As the front desk staff had promised, the pool and gym were first class. There wasn't anyone in the pool, so I took my time leisurely swimming laps in the 25-meter pool, enjoying the warm water, peace and quiet, and the exercise. Before I got addicted to running, I was a swimmer all through junior high, then on a city team, high school, and finally in the Navy. My best stroke was the breast-stroke; I always placed first or second in high school and with the City of Seal Beach. When I was a kid, my brother would go down to the beach with me, and paddle alongside me on his surfboard while I swam in the open ocean, getting faster and stronger, as I fought currents, waves, and the occasional sea critter. Today — I'm not sure why — those fond memories of my brother paddling beside me came flooding back into my mind, even though I hadn't thought about those times in years.

Like I do on so many trips, I ordered room service: a salad, a couple glasses of wine, and garlic bread. I was not really tired, but tonight I just didn't want to socialize. I was melancholy and a bit aloof tonight, and I knew myself well enough to realize that it was best to keep to myself and let my mood blow by. I knew by morning I'd feel better.

I finally turned off the television around 10:00, curled up in a semi-ball, and fell quickly to sleep. I dreamed of airplanes, Dave, running, and fighting bad guys. When I woke up in the morning, the bedspread was tumbled in a big pile on the floor, the sheets were half wadded up, and pillows were thrown about on every corner of the bed.

"Wow that was a rough night. Good morning Lord, get me through this day. Thanks," I said, as I put my feet on the floor, and began getting ready, coffee being the top priority of my morning.

Our 0800 briefing was held in the team leader's room, up on the tenth floor. Unlike me, he had a fabulous view of the airport. I sat down on one of the beds next to Agent Stanton, as introductions were being made around the room. Agent Tony Lopez, our team leader, began filling us in on the purpose of this mission and why it had been organized so quickly.

As background, Agent Lopez stated, "Most of the poor population living in Haiti…for hundreds of years, has suffered under military domination. Most of the money that the Haitian government got was taken from the large poor peasant population. Then the political system began to falter. The Haitian political system is currently in a profound state of crisis, and in 1985 a very large surge of unrest occurred, which led to the fall of the Jean-Claude Duvalier government a few years ago, in February 1986. Since then, a series of short-lived governments have ruled the country."

Agent Lopez continued by saying that our intelligence resources indicated that the political unrest in Haiti was increasing, and that the FAA had been notified that several aircraft hijacking plans had been discovered in recent weeks. Federal air marshal teams were being deployed to fly on all US aircraft operating in and out of Haiti, until the government stabilized. We were one of those teams, who would, over the next ten to twelve days, make daily round trips to and from Haiti. Some of the cadre would depart every morning on American Airlines at 0600, and return in the afternoon at 1440 hours. Other cadre members would depart on Delta Air Lines at 1400 hours and return at 2300 hours. The flights were two hours, and while we were in Haiti, we would stay on the aircraft, with our firearms visible and ready to use.

This tactic was completely different from how we had been trained. We were a covert cadre, displaying arms only when the threat became visible. But in this circumstance, I understood that the threat was already visible, and we needed to make sure that no one was allowed inside the aircraft who was not authorized to be onboard. "Hired to protect" took on a new meaning for me during this briefing.

"Are we ready to fly?" Agent Lopez asked while looking around the room. "Who's got questions?"

Questions were asked and answered, and tactical scenarios were discussed at length. The cadre was smaller than normal, thus allowing for more flights to be protected. It was a necessary tactical decision, and we all understood our mission. I was assigned to the flight leaving at 1400 that afternoon. Earlier in the day, Agent Lopez had asked Agent Stanton to be the assistant team leader for the Delta flight, and Agent Lopez would lead the American Airlines flights. I was one of the air marshals assigned to work for Agent Stanton.

I went back to my room, changed clothes, and headed back downstairs to meet the team. We all grabbed a quick bite to eat in the café at the hotel, and then boarded the hotel shuttle for the short ride to the Delta terminal. The check-in process, circumnavigation of the checkpoint, and crew introductions and briefing were complete. We proceeded to pre-board the aircraft as planned.

I was seated in coach when the passengers started boarding. A very thin older man boarded, and I immediately knew that he was seated in my row. I wasn't sure if he was in the middle seat, or by the window, but he was heading for row twelve, with his thick black Bible in one hand, a brimmed hat in the other, and a disheveled look about him. He looked haggard, sunburnt, and tired, perhaps from too many airplane rides, or life. Either way, he stopped at row twelve, looked at me, stepped into the row, and sat down in the seat next to the window. The flight was completely full; full of crying babies, tired travelers, Haitians heading home, and unbeknownst to most, a team of federal air marshals.

Again, the middle seat was empty. I wondered about this; I either had incredibly good fortune, or nobody wanted to sit next to me. It seems that on more flights than not in the past couple of years, seats were open next to me, rather than filled. Most, that is, except the flight where I had met Dave. I smiled at the thought, and hoped that he too was safe on his travels this week. I scanned the cabin, while pretending to read a magazine, watching for any signs of discontent, or people looking nervous, or scared. The flight attendants served drinks, but no meal service, since the flight was only two hours, so the aisle was empty most of the flight, except for the occasional passenger who needed to use the lavatory.

As we approached Haiti, where the land mass and the sea touched, turbulence made itself known. The captain turned on the seatbelt sign, and the flight attendants ensured that the captain's command was followed. It was a bumpy landing, but any landing was a good landing in my opinion, especially after the trip to India. Many of the passengers clapped their hands when we were safely on the ground.

Once the airplane was parked on the tarmac, stairs were rolled up to the airplane so the passengers could leave. I stood up, began collecting my belongings, and appeared as if I were going to deplane with the rest of the passengers, but I lagged behind, waiting for all of the passengers to deplane. I let the man seated at the window get past me and begin his journey into Port au Prince.

The team gathered in the forward section of the aircraft, waiting for Agent Stanton to tell each team member where they would be standing guard while the aircraft was on the ground.

Agent Stanton assigned another agent, Agent Paul, and me to stand at the bottom of the aircraft boarding stairs, firearms visible; at any cost, we must not let anyone on the aircraft without a valid airline identification badge.

Agent Paul and I deplaned, and as our feet touched the tarmac, we drew our firearms, and stood on each side of the stairs. Since I was a left-handed shooter, I stood on the left side of the stairs, and Agent Paul stayed on the right. It was a tactical maneuver to position ourselves with our firearms closest to the stairs, mainly to protect our firearms if anyone attempted to take them. Everything on this mission was a tactical nightmare: smaller teams, higher threat, overt tactics versus covert, and Mother Nature. As we stood in the hot, humid 83-degree day, I began to perspire, thinking and knowing that there was absolutely no way that Agent Paul and I would remain anonymous now. As we stood guard, gazing at the chain link fence dividing the airport security area from our position, we watched all the people staring back at us, their fingers curled in the links, waiting, watching, and wondering when and where this plane was going. We stood guard for an hour and a half before an airline employee came to tell us that we would be boarding in about ten minutes. That was our signal to holster our firearms, but remain in position until all of the passengers were onboard.

Once the boarding process began, Agent Paul and I stood in the hot Haitian sunshine for another twenty minutes before everyone was onboard, and the cabin crew waved to us to board the aircraft.

As I walked into the cabin, I felt every passenger's eyes boring into me; they knew my purpose, my destination, and that I was armed. I kept my facial features, body language, and stride as severe and purposeful as I could. I wanted everyone on the aircraft to be afraid of me. As I took my seat in the back of the aircraft, the passenger sitting in the middle seat next to me didn't say a word — not a peep. He didn't look at me or acknowledge my presence in any way, shape, or form. *No one is going to mess with me on this flight,* I thought. *I have full command of this situation.*

After landing back in Miami, our team met to debrief, and then went to the bar for drinks before calling it a day. Agent Stanton commended Agent Paul and me for our excellent coverage today, with the highlight of my entry onto the aircraft, and command presence. I tipped my wine glass, and said, "Yes, indeed, you know me. I'm Mad Dog Stewart, and I've been HIRED TO PROTECT."

CPSIA information can be obtained at www.ICGtesting.com
Printed in the USA
BVOW02s1340110314

347306BV00007B/24/P

9 781432 793906